77 FAQs
ABOUT GOD
AND THE BIBLE

JOSH McDOWELL
SEAN McDOWELL

D1007370

HARVEST HOUSE PUBLISHERS
EUGENE, OREGON

Cover by Koechel Peterson & Associates, Inc., Minneapolis, Minnesota

Cover photo © Design Pics / Ron Nickel / Getty Images

77 FAQS ABOUT GOD AND THE BIBLE

Copyright © 2012 by Josh McDowell and Sean McDowell
Published by Harvest House Publishers
Eugene, Oregon 97402
www.harvesthousepublishers.com

Library of Congress Cataloging-in-Publication Data
McDowell, Josh.
   77 FAQs about God and the Bible / Josh McDowell and Sean McDowell.
      p. cm. — (The McDowell apologetics library)
   ISBN 978-0-7369-4924-8 (pbk.)
   ISBN 978-0-7369-4925-5 (eBook)
   1. God (Christianity)—Miscellanea. 2. Bible—Miscellanea. I. McDowell, Sean. II. Title.
   BT103.M325 2012
   239—dc23
                                                                                        2011050764

Printed in the United States of America

12 13 14 15 16 17 18 19 20 / LB-CD / 10 9 8 7 6 5 4 3 2 1

ACKNOWLEDGMENTS

We wish to recognize the following individuals for their valuable contribution to this book.

Dave Bellis, my (Josh's) friend and colleague for 35 years, for collaboration with us on the questions for the book, researching answers, writing the rough draft, and folding in all our edits and revisions to create the final draft. We recognize Dave's insights and general knowledge on the topics in this book and are deeply grateful for his contribution.

Eric Johnson and *Alan Shlemon* for providing helpful insight in their areas of expertise.

Becky Bellis for laboring at the computer to ready the manuscript.

Terry Glaspey of Harvest House for his vision and guidance in shaping the direction and tone of this work.

Paul Gossard of Harvest House for the expert editing and insight he brought to the manuscript completion.

Josh McDowell
Sean McDowell

CONTENTS

QUESTIONS ABOUT THE BIBLE

1.

CAN I HAVE ALL MY
QUESTIONS ANSWERED?

Thoughtful answers to the most frequently asked questions about God and the Bible are sometimes difficult to find. We (Josh and Sean) are attempting to provide you with them. All together, we have spoken over 15,000 times to youth and adult audiences. We have sought to research the issues and questions Christians and non-Christians alike have asked. We have studied what scholars and theologians of the past have said. And it would be nice to say we have found all the answers. But that is simply not the case.

The subject of God and his divine Word is so immense and deep that we have to confess there are far more questions than there are answers. In fact, the more we study and learn about God and the Bible, the more we realize how little we actually do know. Yet this doesn't mean we are left without good reasons for what we believe.

There are many questions on the subjects of God and the Bible that have satisfying answers. But to some people they may not be satisfying—in fact, they may seem foolish to those who do not believe. Even the apostle Paul said the message of the cross is foolishness to those who don't believe (1 Corinthians 1:18)! Many of the questions we are answering are spiritual questions that require spiritual answers. If you accept only "secular" answers, you may be disappointed.

So on many occasions we will be asking you to see the answer from God's perspective, because that is when we receive true insight and wisdom. When we see life and its dilemmas from a godlike viewpoint we gain insight and direction. Our hope is that you will find such answers in this book. At the same time we are dealing with some very difficult questions—questions that have been contemplated for centuries. And some of these answers, while satisfying to a point, remain incomplete. Sometimes we must accept that there are issues and situations God knows but that remain partially or wholly a mystery to us humans. This does not mean

Christianity is a matter of *blind* faith. But it is important to recognize our own human limitations.

So no—not all of your questions about God and the Bible can be answered in this or any other book. But we will do our best to address every question honestly and provide answers that are as clear and practical as possible. However, the key in getting real answers to the tough questions of life is in the approach. In his wisdom, King Solomon understood this approach, and he shared it with us in the second chapter of Proverbs. Real answers come from gaining understanding and wisdom from God.

> My child, listen to me and treasure my instructions. Tune your ears to wisdom, and concentrate on understanding. Cry out for insight and understanding. Search for them as you would for lost money or hidden treasure. Then you will understand what it means to fear the LORD, and you will gain knowledge of God. For the LORD grants wisdom! From his mouth come knowledge and understanding. He grants a treasure of good sense to the godly. He is their shield, protecting those who walk with integrity. He guards the paths of justice and protects those who are faithful to him.
>
> Then you will understand what is right, just, and fair, and you will know how to find the right course of action every time (Proverbs 2:1-9 NLT).

QUESTIONS
ABOUT GOD

2.

WHY DOES GOD SEEM
HIDDEN FROM US?

What if I (Sean) told you I owned a brand-new Lamborghini and it was sitting in my garage right now? If you knew me you would probably say I couldn't afford such a high-priced car on a high-school teacher's salary. Of course, you'd be right. But all you would have to do is call my hand and say, "Show me the Lamborghini." And if I couldn't produce the goods, I would be a fraud.

It's a little different when it comes to producing "the goods" on God. We just can't pray a prayer or snap our fingers and presto!—God appears and dispels any question about his existence. To be truthful, even that might not persuade some people to believe in him. But the fact is, God in a real sense remains hidden to us as a *material* being. The Scripture says, "God is Spirit, so those who worship him must worship in spirit and in truth" (John 4:24). And as a spirit, God is invisible to us (see 1 Timothy 1:17). You see, he is on another plane of existence than we humans. We are not meant to see him in all his awesome power and might. He told Moses, "You may not look directly at my face, for no one may see me and live" (Exodus 33:20).

Actually God is hidden from us because he is a perfectly holy God (Isaiah 54:5 and Revelation 4:8) and we as humans are imperfect and unholy (Romans 5:12). We are contaminated with evil, and Scripture says God's "eyes are too pure to look on evil; you cannot tolerate wrong doing" (Habakkuk 1:13 NIV).*

The spirit form of God is too much for us sinful mortals to stand, and he must remain hidden from us. Yet God wants a relationship with his creation, and he has enabled us to know him through the sacrificial death of Christ, which atones for our sin. Christ's atoning for sin means that Jesus paid the "wages of sin" for us, which was death, and that he "ransomed" us out of the "prison" of death. (See Romans 6:23 and 1 Peter 1:18-19.) He

---

* See "What Is God Really Like?" on page 39 and "What Causes People to Sin Today?" on page 54.

also reveals himself to us through creation (Romans 1:18-21), our moral consciences (Romans 2:14-15), his Word (2 Timothy 3:16-17), the church (Ephesians 1:23), history (1 Samuel 17:46-47), and through the indwelling of his Holy Spirit in our lives (Romans 8:9-11). God may be hidden from us in a material, physical sense, but he is very much evident in the life of a child of God, who has been redeemed through Christ.

Of course God revealed himself to us in the person of Jesus Christ when he was here on earth. There are many evidences or proofs we will offer in this book to support an intelligent faith that Jesus in fact was God in the flesh. Jesus and the apostles clearly stated that he was the revelation of God to us. (See John 1:1-14; 14:8-11; Colossians 2:9; and Hebrews 1.) So while God may be hidden to us in the material world, he has still revealed himself to us in a substantial way.

And on one level the hidden aspect of God is not a negative thing. His hiddenness can have a very positive result. He told the children of Israel, "If you look for me in earnest, you will find me when you seek me. I will be found by you" (Jeremiah 29:13-14 NLT). Jesus said, "Seek and you will find" (Luke 11:9 NIV). As with hidden treasure, God wants us to seek and search and discover all the riches that his relationship with us offers. There is mystery to that which is hidden from us. And that mystery can deepen our desire to know the hidden riches of God.

3.

DOESN'T BELIEVING IN GOD REQUIRE FAITH?

Although there are a number of arguments for God's existence—and we will cover those in this book—when it comes down to it, isn't believing in God really a matter of faith? In fact, don't all religious questions belong in the realm of faith?

Faith is vitally important, yet many people misunderstand it, thinking it means you throw away your mind and just believe blindly. That is not what biblical faith is about.

ASSURANCE AND CONVICTION

The Bible says, "Faith is the assurance of things hoped for, the conviction of things not seen" (Hebrews 11:1 NASB). A good question to ask is, "Where do the *assurance* and *conviction* of our faith come from?" They come from knowledge or evidence of the things hoped for or not seen. It is your knowledge of something that allows you to trust in it. And seeing the evidence gives your faith confidence. So biblical faith isn't a blind faith that operates without any reason to believe—rather, it looks at the evidence. In fact that is one of the reasons the apostles of Jesus recorded many of the miraculous signs performed by Jesus: "These [signs] are written down so that you may continue to believe that Jesus is the Messiah" (John 20:31).

Here is an example: You exercise faith every time you fly in an airplane. You may not even see the pilot, but you place your faith in him or her to safely fly the plane. You probably have not seen the expert engineers, machinists, and craftsmen who built the aircraft, but you believe the plane you are flying on is airworthy. So where do you get the assurance you are traveling safely? You have no doubt placed your faith in the knowledge of the airline's record of performance and the FAA rules that regulate and monitor the airline industry. There is overwhelming evidence that airline travel is safe. And that knowledge of the evidence gives assurance and conviction to your belief.

The point is, your faith is based upon knowledge about the airline company and its strict rules of operation. You have gained assurance based on an intelligent or knowledgeable faith or on personal experience. Your faith isn't a blind faith that requires no information or evidence at all. Believing something without clear evidence is like taking a leap into the dark; acting on faith that is rooted in clear evidence is like stepping into the light.

In the Old Testament, God sent Moses to Pharaoh, the leader of Egypt. God worked miraculous acts to convince Pharaoh to release the children of Israel. Finally he relented. But the evidence of God's might had a profound impact on Israel. "When the people of Israel saw the mighty power that the LORD had unleashed against the Egyptians they were filled with awe before him. They put their faith in the LORD and his servant Moses" (Exodus 14:31).

But evidence of God isn't always that pronounced. Most of the time he is hidden from us in the material world and we must continue to believe anyway. Yet that doesn't mean we can't be assured or have deep conviction about him based on evidence. In this book, we will provide evidence for God and answer questions about what he is like, and that will help give us a firm faith.

FAITH AND EVIDENCE WORK TOGETHER

No matter how exhaustive or convincing the evidence is, we still must exercise faith. When I (Sean) married my wife, Stephanie, I didn't have exhaustive or complete knowledge about her. I couldn't know absolutely 100 percent that she was a person of integrity. That, of course, was important to me because I wanted to marry a person who loved me enough to be faithful and true to me. But during our dating period I actually came to know her for the person she was. So I gained sufficient evidence to make a wise, informed decision on the moral character of the person I eventually married. Yet it still took a step of faith for both of us to place our love and trust in each other.

You will seldom, if ever, have exhaustive evidence for believing in anything. But you can find sufficient evidence to establish that what you believe is credible and objectively true. When it comes to God, he wants a relationship with us more than anything, and the key to a relationship is trust. So the more we know about his character, his heart, and his motivations and desires, the deeper our convictions will grow and the stronger our faith will be in his person.

Faith and evidence work hand in hand that way. For example, when trying times come into your life, your faith in God can be tested. Tragedies like a devastating storm that destroys your home, the loss of a job, or a terrible disease that takes a loved one from you can test your faith to the limit. It's easy at those times to ask, "Why?" And sometimes there is no satisfying answer. We can be tempted to ask, "Doesn't God see what's happening? Doesn't he care? Why doesn't he do something about it?" The Scripture tell us, "These trials are only to test your faith, to show that it is strong and pure. It is being tested as fire tests and purifies gold—and your faith is far more precious to God than mere gold" (1 Peter 1:7 NLT).

Why is your faith so "precious" and so important to God? Because a "strong and pure" faith in him is a faith full of knowledge of who he is. More than anything God wants us to know him for the true God that he is. He wants us to rely on him during trying times. He wants us to know he is there for us no matter what. Jesus prayed to his Father God and said, "This is the way to have eternal life—to know you, the only true God, and Jesus Christ, the one you sent to earth" (John 17:3). To know God is to trust our lives to him. The more that we come to know him the more we can place our complete trust in him.*

Most people who know my (Josh's) personal story know that I set out to disprove Christianity. I wanted to uncover evidence that would show that the Bible and its incredible stories were a fraud. Of course, my examination of the evidences of Christ's deity, his resurrection, and the reliability of Scripture proved otherwise. And so people assume I came to Christ through the intellectual route.

Truth is, all the evidence I have documented in my books did not bring me to a relationship with Christ. The convincing evidence certainly got my attention. But what drew me to God was a firsthand knowledge of his love. I saw love between a group of Jesus-followers who devoted themselves to loving God and one another. And God demonstrated his love to me through them. When I experienced his loving me through these Christ-followers, something happened. That is when I placed my faith in him, and through the power of his Holy Spirit my life was transformed. I exercised a knowledgeable faith in a God who loved me enough to die for me.

---

* See "What Is God Really Like?" on page 39.

The Bible says, "It is impossible to please God without faith. Anyone who wants to come to him must believe that God exists and that he rewards those who sincerely seek him" (Hebrews 11:6). If your faith in God is weak, this book is intended to strengthen it. If your faith in God is strong, this book will make it even stronger. The more you look at the evidence of God's existence—who he really is, what he is really like—and clarify for yourself the many misunderstandings about him, the more your faith in him will deepen and grow.

4.

IS IT WRONG TO HAVE DOUBTS ABOUT GOD?

God wants us to believe in him. He wants us to place our faith in him and believe he has our best interest at heart. So is it wrong to have some doubts creep in—doubts over what God has to say about what he has commanded in the Bible or how we are to live out the Christian life?

The faith of the great John the Baptist seemed to waver when he was imprisoned and things were looking grim. He sent his followers to ask Jesus, "Are you the Messiah we've been expecting, or should we keep looking for someone else?" (Matthew 11:3).

Remember this is the man who had said, "I testify that he [Jesus] is the Chosen One of God" (John 1:34). But after John was thrown into prison he must have wondered why Jesus wasn't coming to rescue him. Like many of us do when faced with difficulties, John the Baptist experienced doubts.

When other disciples of Jesus were questioning who he actually was, he told them to "believe that I am in the Father and the Father is in me. Or at least believe because of the work you have seen me do" (John 14:11). Jesus wasn't put off because his followers had some doubts or wanted some proof. He appealed to evidence to establish that he was who he claimed to be. God wants our faith in him to be assured and become deepened by our convictions. And having some uncertainties at times isn't necessarily wrong. Like John the Baptist, we sometimes lack sufficient evidence to support our faith. And so, seeking to know why we believe what we believe can strengthen our faith and is by no means wrong.

Many of our doubts can be put aside as our faith becomes more intelligent about the evidences—knowing why we believe. But the evidences are not limited to things like Christ's resurrection, his deity, the reliability of Scripture, and so on. There are also evidences about God's character and nature that will support our faith and remove our doubts.

A man came to Jesus hoping Jesus could heal his son. The man said,

> "Have mercy on us and help us, if you can." "What do you mean, 'If I can'?" Jesus asked. "Anything is possible if a person believes." The father instantly cried out, "I do believe, but help me overcome my unbelief!" (Mark 9:22-24).

This man had faith, but he wanted help from Jesus not to doubt that the Master would heal his son. This father had probably heard stories of the miracle-working teacher. He may have personally known the blind man who got his sight back because of Jesus. He may have had a neighbor who was among the thousands who were fed by the five loaves of bread and two fish that Jesus blessed. So the man no doubt believed Jesus had the power to heal his son, but the big question for him was, *Will Jesus care enough to heal my son?*

Sometimes our doubts revolve around our faith in God's nature and compassion. Does he care enough about me to heal my child? Does he want to meet my material needs? Will he keep me safe? It is important to know the evidences of his caring heart to help remove our doubts.*

Jesus was once taking a nap on a boat while crossing the Sea of Galilee with his disciples. A fierce storm came through and the disciples thought they were going to drown, so they woke Jesus up. He rebuked the foul weather and stopped the storm. "Then he asked them, 'Where is your faith?'" (Luke 8:25). It appears the storm is what occupied his disciples' minds and emotions. And that kept them from trusting their situation to Jesus. Of course he wanted them to believe he was the One who had the power to calm the storm and who cared enough to keep them safe. He wanted them to have faith in him.

Jesus also told his disciples not to worry about their need for food and clothing. He said God took care of the birds and the flowers and "he will certainly care for you. Why do you have so little faith?" (Luke 12:28). Again, Jesus wanted his followers to focus on the caring and providing nature of his heart. Yet the worries of life and all its insecurities could easily cause them to doubt. They can cause us to doubt too.

Placing our focus on the providing and protecting nature of God's

---

* See "What Is God Really Like?" on page 39.

heart allows us to follow Peter's admonition to "give all your worries and cares to God, for he cares about you" (1 Peter 5:7). The future is unknown and our lives are full of uncertainty and insecurity. And while it is in our nature to question how things are going to turn out, when we add the knowledge or evidence of the caring heart of God to our faith, our doubts can be removed. So while it may not be wrong to have some doubts about God, he wants to remove them so we can trust him for whatever comes our way.

What Kind of Proofs Are
There that God Exists?

The majority of people in America and around the world believe there is a God. When asked for good reasons why they believe that, many simply say, "A beautiful and exquisitely crafted world like this couldn't have come into being by chance." And they are right. But how do you formulate that intuitive answer into an argument or proof that God actually exists?

The Scripture says, "Ever since the world was created, people have seen the earth and sky. Through everything God made, they can clearly see his invisible qualities—his eternal power and divine nature" (Romans 1:20). God doesn't have to materialize to prove his existence—his invisible qualities are here and they do provide sufficient proof that he exists.

EVERYTHING FITS

I (Sean) grew up in the mountain town of Julian, California. I have always enjoyed walking the mountain trails and hiking in the woods. I have introduced my young children to exploring the forests.

Let's assume I'm out hiking with my son Scottie. About two hours into our hike Scottie says, "Dad, I'm getting tired. And I'm thirsty." Right then we catch sight of what looks like a structure through the trees. As we approach, we see a picture-perfect cabin in the middle of the woods. The door has been left wide open.

Scottie and I make our way into the cabin. To our amazement my favorite music is playing. Scottie's favorite Wii video game appears on the TV screen. We see a sign on the refrigerator that says, *Favorite Drinks Inside*. Scottie runs over, opens the refrigerator, and takes out a Sierra Mist. "Can you believe this, Dad?" he blurts out just before guzzling down his drink. This would all be just too amazing, right?

What would you conclude by all this? Could these circumstances have come about by sheer chance? It would seem that someone had to have known we were coming and designed the cabin, the music, game, and drinks with us in mind.

────────────

While this fantastic cabin discovery is just a story, the reality is that Planet Earth is even more amazing and fantastic. As with the cabin illustration, it is as if someone carefully prepared our world exactly with us in mind. Certain laws of nature rest within very narrowly defined parameters that allow humans to exist here.

Scientists conservatively estimate there are at least 18 physical laws that work in perfect harmony in order for the universe and Planet Earth to be suitable for complex life. For example, there are the laws of gravity, conservation of energy, thermodynamics, strong nuclear forces, electromagnetic forces, and so on. If any of these laws varied ever so slightly, life would not be possible in our universe.

Consider the strong nuclear force. This is the force that holds the nuclei—centers—of atoms together. The protons and neutrons of the atom within the nuclei exchange subparticles. The protons are then bound together by the strong force, even though their positive charges would normally repel each other. And the atom stays intact.

To see one of the results of the strong force, take the sun's production of nuclear energy, for example. Our sun "burns" and produces energy to sustain Planet Earth by fusing hydrogen atoms together. And when two such atoms fuse, 0.7 percent of their mass is converted into energy. But what if the percentage of matter converted to energy was slightly smaller? If the conversion was just 0.6 percent instead of 0.7 percent, the proton could not bond to the neutron and the universe would consist only of hydrogen. There would be no Planet Earth for us to inhabit, nor would there be a sun to warm it.

And what if the matter converted to energy was just a bit larger, say 0.8 percent? The fusion would happen so quickly that no hydrogen could survive. And this would also mean that life as we know it could not exist. Our universe is so fine-tuned that the tiny hydrogen atoms, when fusing, must give up exactly between 0.6 percent and 0.8 percent of their mass in the form of energy![1]

There are dozens of such examples that demonstrate that our universe is finely tuned to an incredible degree. It is unthinkable that it originated "by chance." It is as if some Intelligent Agent prepared Planet Earth with a welcome sign that said, "I made this specifically for you."

———————

Those who believe in the God of the Bible are not surprised by the discovery of the fine-tuning of the universe. In fact, this is exactly what we *would* expect to find if he exists. The Bible says, "He (Jesus) sustains everything by the mighty power of his command" (Hebrews 1:3). The idea that "luck" or "chance" accounts for the creation of the world in all its complexity and precision requires far more faith than believing that there is a Creator God who prepared it just for us.

> The heavens proclaim the glory of God. The skies display his craftsmanship. Day after day they continue to speak; night after night they make him known. They speak without a sound or word; their voice is never heard. Yet their message has gone throughout the earth, and their words to all the world (Psalm 19:1-4).

The invisible God has given us proof of his existence within the known universe—in what we can see with our eyes and reason out with our minds. The evidences of God's existence can be examined in what we call "arguments" for his existence. Four key ones are the first-cause argument, the design argument, the moral law argument, and the personal experience argument. These four will be discussed within the next four questions.

6.

WHAT IS THE FIRST-CAUSE ARGUMENT FOR GOD'S EXISTENCE?

Even as a young boy I (Sean) often wondered how everything that existed came into being. I thought if the universe had a beginning then something must have brought the universe into existence. And that something, it seemed to me, must have been God. This is the essence of the *first-cause argument* for the existence of God, also referred to as the *cosmological argument*.

The premise is that everything that begins to exist must have a cause. So if you go back in time far enough you will find the first cause—and that cause will be Creator God. Actually this argument has three premises:

1. Whatever begins to exist has a cause.

2. The universe began to exist.

3. Therefore the universe has a cause.

The first premise works from the simple logic that something now exists (our universe) and that something cannot spring from nothing. It's true that the combination of things can produce new things—for instance, two parts hydrogen and one part oxygen equals water—but that is not something coming out of nothing. The conclusion then is that whatever begins to exist has a cause—and the universe did indeed begin to exist.

The second premise, in part, makes its point from the second law of thermodynamics. That law states that the universe is expending all of its useful energy. So if the universe had no beginning—was infinitely old— then it would already have used up its useful energy. For example, our sun is burning its energy and will one day burn out. Therefore it, along with all the stars in the universe, had a beginning. (There is other scientific evidence that the universe began to exist, including the red-shift, the cosmic background microwave radiation, and the implications of Einstein's General Theory of Relativity.)

The last premise builds on the previous two: the universe has a cause.

The question then arises, "Who caused the cause?" We can derive our answer from the origins of time, space, and matter. It is logical to conclude that since time, space, and matter did not exist before the beginning of the universe, then the "cause" of the universe had to be timeless, spaceless, and immaterial. Further, this "cause" could not be physical or subject to natural law, since that would presuppose that its existence involved time, space, and matter. These, taken together, lead us to conclude that this timeless, spaceless, immaterial "cause" was God.

———

The first-cause argument is a strong one. In a nutshell, since the universe had a beginning, then something or someone had to cause it. And that someone was God. This may not get us all the way to the God of Abraham, Isaac, and Jacob, but it does rule out atheism as a plausible explanation for the origin of the universe.

7.

WHAT IS THE DESIGN ARGUMENT FOR GOD'S EXISTENCE?

The *design argument* is also called the *teleological argument*. It makes the point that life, the laws of nature, and the whole of the universe demonstrate immense specified complexity, the mark of design—therefore the universe must have come from an Intelligent Designer.

Some time ago I (Sean) collaborated with Dr. William Dembski in writing a book entitled *Understanding Intelligent Design.** In it we covered the many facets of the arguments for intelligent design. The remaining portion of this answer is drawn from that book.

If you have ever visited Disneyland or Disney World, at the entry you have probably noticed the bed of flowers laid out on a sloping bank. Its colors and pattern form a clear resemblance to Mickey Mouse. No one would attribute that gardening marvel to mere chance. Why? First, flowers of those varieties and colors don't just grow by chance to form the shape and color of the famous Mickey Mouse. The numerous types of flowers and the sophistication of their placement clearly indicate *complexity*. Complexity in this sense is the same as saying it is highly improbable that these flowers randomly grew there or were positioned so intricately.

Second, besides being complex, the floral arrangement is laid out in a very specific manner. Certain flowers make up the eyes, others the nose, and yet others the mouth and the renowned ears. The image exhibits an independently given pattern—it's therefore *specified*.

This combination of complexity (or improbability) and specificity (or independently imposed patterning) is called *specified complexity*. Specified complexity is a marker of intelligence. Like a fingerprint or a signature, specified complexity identifies the activity of an intelligent agent. The huge flower beds at Disneyland and Disney World exhibit specified complexity and lead us to believe an intelligent gardener was their cause. Does the same pattern exist within nature?

---

* Harvest House Publishers, 2008. For more about *Understanding Intelligent Design,* see the back of this book.

WHAT A SINGLE LIVING CELL DECLARES

The more specified complexity a thing displays—that is, the more complex it is and the more its form obviously follows specific patterns—the more it points to an intelligent designer. Take, for example, the building block of human life—a single living cell. Does it have specified complexity?

> Let's briefly look at a cell magnified a billion times. On its surface we find millions of openings, like portholes in a ship. But these are not mere portholes. They regulate the flow of materials in and out of the cell. Cells exhibit nano-engineering on a scale and sophistication that scientists have hardly begun to scratch. Francis Crick, one of the co-discoverers of DNA's structure, described the cell as "a minute factory, bustling with rapid, organized chemical activity." That was in the early 1980s. Scientists now think of the cell as an automated city.
>
> Inside the cell we find a host of raw materials maneuvered back and forth by robot-like machines all working in unison. In fact, many different objects move in perfect unison through seemingly endless conduits. The level of control in these choreographed movements is truly mind-blowing. And this is just *one* cell. In larger organisms, cells must work together for the proper function of organs such as hearts, eyes, livers, and ears, and these in turn must work together for the life of the organism.
>
> If we peer further inside the cell, we find coils of DNA that store the information necessary to construct proteins. Proteins themselves are remarkably complex molecular systems. A typical protein is composed of a few hundred amino acids arranged in a precisely ordered sequence that then folds into a highly organized three-dimensional structure. That structure enables the protein to perform its function inside the cell.
>
> Biologists today cannot even describe the activities inside the cell without comparing it to machines and other feats of modern engineering. The reason is that nearly every feature of our own advanced technology can be found in the cell.[2]

As we carefully observe the inner workings of the cell, one thing becomes apparent: There is complexity and sophistication that dwarfs human technological innovation today. This is why more and more scientists are concluding that the best explanation for the cell is intelligent design.

LIFE REQUIRES VAST AMOUNTS OF INFORMATION

The key feature of life is information. Life, even the simplest of bacterial cells, requires vast amounts of information to function. Cellular information is stored in DNA. The DNA in one cell in the human body holds the equivalent of roughly 8000 books of information. A typical human body has about 100 trillion cells, each of which has a DNA strand that could be uncoiled to about three meters in length. Thus, if all the DNA in an adult human were strung together, it would stretch from Earth to the sun and back around 70 times![3]

Supposing there were no Intelligent Designer—how would the needed information for life be assembled? The typical answer Darwinists come up with is this: Given enough time, matter, and chance, anything can happen.

But how much time, matter, and chance are actually available? As early as 1913, the French mathematician Émile Borel argued that a million monkeys typing ten hours a day would be exceedingly unlikely to reproduce the books in the world's libraries. The universe is very old and enormous, according to Borel, but not old and big enough for something that unlikely.

> Let's narrow Borel's scope. Instead of focusing on many books, let's consider the works of Shakespeare. Here is the question: How many monkeys and how much time would be required to reproduce one of the works of Shakespeare, or even just a few lines?

> Work has been done on this question by MIT computational quantum physicist Seth Lloyd. According to Lloyd, in the known physical universe, chance is capable of producing only 400 bits of prespecified information (this is equivalent to a string of 400 zeroes and ones). This amounts to a sequence of 82 ordinary letters and spaces. Therefore, the longest initial segment of Hamlet's soliloquy that the entire universe—given

its size and purported multibillion-year history—could by chance produce is the following two lines:

TO BE, OR NOT TO BE, THAT IS THE QUESTION.
WHETHER 'TIS NOBLER IN THE MIND TO SUFFER...

Clearly, the phenomenon of chance is limited in its ability to explain certain features of the universe. All the chance in the known universe can't randomly type more than two lines of Shakespeare, much less an entire book.[4]

If chance operating over time cannot create enough information for two lines of Shakespeare, how could it ever create the specified complexity of even a single primitive cell? A single cell requires hundreds of thousands of bits of information precisely sequenced in its DNA. So those who deny an Intelligent Designer have the impossible task of explaining how the information (specified complexity) in even a simple living organism could arise from an unguided, blind process. Life simply requires too much information for it to have occurred randomly. For example:

The information-storage capacity of DNA far surpasses even the most powerful electronic memory systems known today. Molecular biologist Michael Denton notes that, for all the different types of organisms *that have ever lived*, the necessary information in their DNA for the construction of their proteins "could be held in a teaspoon and there would still be room left for all the information in every book ever written." But DNA does not just store information. In combination with other cellular systems, it also processes information. Hence Bill Gates likens DNA to a computer program, though far more advanced than any software humans have invented.

This is why intelligent design best explains the information content of DNA. Imagine you are walking on the beach and notice the message "Sean loves Stephanie" inscribed in the sand. What would you conclude? You might think Sean, Stephanie, or some gossipy stranger wrote it, but it would never cross your mind to attribute it to chance, necessity, or some combination of the two. Wind, water, and sand simply do not generate meaningful information. The most reasonable inference is that it is a product of intelligent design. If we justifiably infer a mind behind a simple message of 15 characters, then inferring an intelligence for the origin of the cell—which requires hundreds of thousands bits of information—is fully justified.[5]

When we look at the incredible complexity and design all around us we are faced with a choice. Either the entire universe, down to a single living cell, was designed, or it developed by some combination of chance and the laws of nature. The cosmos is either a product of Intelligent Design or a cosmic fluke.

8.

What Is the Moral Law Argument for God's Existence?

Every human culture known to man has had a moral law. We find it in the records of past cultures as well as in all present societies. And the morality of all these societies is surprisingly similar, no matter how widely separated by time, geography, cultural development, or religious belief. The morality defined in the Jewish Ten Commandments, the Babylonian Code of Hammurabi, the Chinese Tao, and the Christian New Testament differs in detail and emphasis but not in essence.

For example, some societies allow individuals to kill to avenge a wrong, while others insist that all execution is the prerogative of the state. Some societies allow freedom in premarital sexual relationships or permit men to take more than one wife, while others forbid such behavior. But all have rules that say people cannot kill others at will or engage in sex with just anyone they want. These laws protect human life. They are rules that govern marriage and family relationships, condemn stealing, and encourage doing good to others.

Throughout history some societies have enforced morality strictly, while others have been lax on one or more points. And within any society there have been people who resisted the imposition of morality on their behavior. When a significant number of these people gain enough power or support for their position, a significant aberration to the universal moral sense can then occur, as it did in Hitler's Germany or in the acceptance of killing female babies in some Asian countries. Usually these aberrations have been short-lived because elements within or outside the society became outraged enough to rise up and stop the aberrant behavior. But despite such variations and distortions, the same basic sense of morality appears wherever humans live together. It's as if many different orchestras are playing from the same score but adapting the harmonies to fit their own instruments.

WHAT'S THE EXPLANATION?

How can we explain a moral code that is so consistently present in all societies? How do we explain a sense of morality that gives virtually every sane person on the planet an innate sense of right and wrong? Why should a moral sense exist at all?[6] Without appeal to a higher source, namely God, what could account for the moral sense that is common to the entire human race through all of history? Where else could morals have come from? If we say our moral intuitions have an origin in a process of blind chance, such as evolution, then morality is a random trick of nature to get us to obey. It follows, then, that morality has no objective basis, and our deep intuitions about certain behavior being objectively wrong are mistaken. Is that a price you are willing to pay? We think there is a better explanation.

An objective, universal, and constant standard of truth and morality points to an existence of a personal and moral God.

> In *The Brothers Karamazov*, Russian novelist Fyodor Dostoyevsky aptly observed, "If there is no immortality of the soul, there can be no virtue and therefore everything is permissible." In other words, if God does not exist as the foundation of morality, then *anything goes*. This doesn't mean atheists or other nonbelievers will necessarily act more immorally than believers, but it does mean we lose an objective basis by which to make moral judgments. If God does not exist then we lose the right to judge the Nazis and anyone else with whom we disagree morally. They believed they were right. We think they were wrong. Without a higher law above humanity, who gets to decide moral truth? If there is no greater source above human beings, then the existence of morality is an inexplicable illusion.[7]

Yet if God exists, then we have a ground for objective morality. We *ought* to be truthful because God is true and faithful. We *ought* to do loving acts because God is love. Morality stems from the character and nature of God and is binding on his creation. The reality of objective moral laws points to the existence of a Moral Lawgiver. Only God's existence and character can properly account for objective morality.

CAN THERE BE AN INDEPENDENT MORALITY?

However, some argue that morality can exist independently of God.

They contend we don't need a God in order to be good—or evil. Yet this assertion presents a problem: How do you define good or evil without some transcendent moral standard? Evil, for example, has traditionally been understood as the perversion of good. Just as crookedness implies a standard of straight, evil implies a standard of good. C.S. Lewis famously said that to complain that a stick is bent makes sense only in light of the concept of straight. Similarly, there can be evil only if there is first good.

But if there is no God, then what is *good*? Without God, we are all left to figure out the meaning of good for ourselves, and the concept of objective good disappears. Good becomes a relative term, for it is simply whatever each of us wants it to be at a given moment, or whatever evolution has blindly wired us to believe.

The universally recognized existence of objective moral values is a strong reason for believing in God. Consider this simple argument:

1. If objective moral values exist, God must exist.

2. Objective moral values exist.

3. Therefore, God must exist.

We know that objective moral values do exist. We don't need to be persuaded that, for example, torturing babies for fun is wrong. All reasonable people know this. Therefore, since moral values do exist, then God must exist as well. This moral law argument provides a strong defense of the assertion that a God of moral character does in fact exist.

9

WHAT IS THE PERSONAL EXPERIENCE ARGUMENT FOR GOD'S EXISTENCE?

Not long after I (Josh) became a Christian I was in a debate with the head of the history department at a Midwestern university. I was telling him how my new relationship with God gave me meaning and purpose. He interrupted me with, "McDowell, are you trying to tell me that you believe in God and he has really changed that much about your life? Give me some specifics." After listening to me explain for 45 minutes, he finally said, "Okay, okay—that's enough!"

People have asked me, "How do you know you became a Christian?" "How do you know God is real?" For one, he changed my life. This transformation is one way that I'm assured of the validity of my conversion and the existence of a real and personal God.

I'm sure you have heard people speak of the "bolt of lightning" that hit them when they had their first religious experience. Well, it wasn't that dramatic for me. After I prayed, nothing happened. I mean *nothing*. And I still haven't sprouted wings or a halo. In fact, after I made my commitment to God, I felt worse. I actually felt I was about to throw up. *Oh no—what have I gotten sucked into now?* I wondered. I really felt I had gone off the deep end (and I'm sure some people think I did!).[8]

The change in my life was not immediate, but it was real. Because of what happened in the time 6 to 18 months after my conversion, I knew I had not gone off the deep end. I had experienced God, and that had changed everything.

A personal experience with God is evidence of his reality. Some people might challenge this assertion, saying that such an experience could easily be an illusion or an emotional or psychological fantasy. But those who have genuinely experienced encounters similar to what Paul the apostle experienced on the Damascus road know better. They know it is real. Such experiences are one of many affirmations of Paul's statement: "Now that you belong to Christ, you are the true children of Abraham. You are his heirs, and now all the promises God gave to him belong to you" (Galatians 3:29 NLT).

———————

A personal experience of God by itself may not be convincing evidence for others, but that does not make it less real. In combination with added evidences or arguments for his existence, a personal testimony to his reality can provide a powerful witness that he "exists and that he rewards those who earnestly seek him" (Hebrews 11:6 NIV).

10.

IF GOD CAUSED EVERYTHING, THEN WHO OR WHAT CAUSED GOD?

Although there may be credible evidence for God's existence, a major question still remains: Who or what caused God? It seems everything that exists had to have a beginning sometime, so when did God begin, and who or what caused him to begin?

In our discussion of the first-cause argument for the existence of God, you may remember it has three premises:

1. Whatever begins to exist has a cause.

2. The universe began to exist.

3. Therefore the universe has a cause.

It is important to clarify that we did not assert that *everything that exists needs a cause*. Rather, everything that *begins* to exist must have a cause.

So the short answer to "Who or what caused God?" is "Nothing." God is eternal, which means he has life without beginning or end. There was never a moment that God didn't exist, nor will he ever end. And because God has always existed, he doesn't need a cause. This is not special pleading by Christians, for the very definition of God implies a being that is self-existent. If God could be caused to exist, then he would not be God! You see, we can only consistently ask what caused things that can in principle be caused, such as chairs, books, and computers. But God, since he is by definition uncaused, is not the type of entity that can be caused. Therefore, the question "What caused God?" is actually meaningless.

When you stop to think about it, our finite minds cannot comprehend or even express how something or someone has always existed. We tend to think everything had to have a beginning. But think of this: "If the world had never been created, would it be true that 1+1 = 2?" Yes, of course. We can understand that such things as mathematical truths and the laws of logic have always existed and are therefore uncaused.

While our minds cannot fathom *how* God has always existed, this does not mean it is illogical to believe *that* it is so. We naturally sense that something outside of our universe had to cause it to come into existence. And the eternal Creator God is the most reasonable explanation. "Have you never heard?" Isaiah asked. "Have you never understood? The LORD is the everlasting God" (Isaiah 40:28).

11.

WHAT IS GOD REALLY LIKE?

The Bible says that God is Spirit (John 4:24) and that no one has ever seen him and lived (Exodus 33:20). So then how can we, being human and not spirit, ever know what he is like?

While it is true that God is hidden from us in many ways,* he has still to a great extent revealed himself to us. He has revealed himself in all of creation. When we see the world around us we get a glimpse of God's creative nature, his infinity of tastes, and his incomprehensible immenseness.

God has also revealed himself to us in Scripture. Through the reliable written Word of God we get deep insights into

1. his infinite characteristics

2. his relational heart

3. his holy nature

And because he has revealed himself to us in the person of Jesus Christ we see God with skin on. We are able to see in a very powerful way just how he wants to relate to us and what he is like relationally. Each of these dimensions of God gives us a greater understanding of what he is really like.

GOD'S INFINITE CHARACTERISTICS

One of the first things we know of God is that he is infinite, which is far beyond our comprehension as finite humans. What does the Scripture tell us?

God is eternal, meaning he possesses an infinite life that is without beginning or end (see Isaiah 40:28). God created time and he involves himself within time, but he exists eternally, outside of time. There was never a moment when he didn't exist, nor will he ever end. We really can't grasp

---

* See "Why Does God Seem Hidden from Us?" on page 13.

the concept of an eternal, self-existing being, but that is part of what God is like.

God is all-powerful. The Bible reveals a God who is almighty—what is called *omnipotent*. If he wants to do something—anything—he can do it. King David said, "How great is our LORD! His power is absolute" (Psalm 147:5). The Almighty God as Sovereign of the universe has the power to know the future and cause it to happen:

> I am God, and there is none like me. Only I can tell you the
> future before it even happens. Everything I plan will come to
> pass, for I do whatever I wish (Isaiah 46:9-10).

God is ever-present. His knowledge and power have no limits—which is why we say God is *omnipresent*. Again, as finite beings we cannot imagine a being that can be ever-present both within and beyond our universe of time and space (see Jeremiah 23:23-24). Yet that is part of what God is like.

God does not change. By his very nature he can be counted on—what is called *immutable*. This means he will not waver or lie. He will always do what he says he will do (see Psalm 102:26-27 and Numbers 23:19). That he is unchanging means he infinitely remains constant, firm, and secure—you can trust whatever he is because he will always be that.

God knows all. He has infinite knowledge. He knows everything past, present, and future—what is called *omniscient* (see Isaiah 46:9-10 and Psalm 139:1). Take everything there is to know within the known universe, for however long it has existed, and that wouldn't even scratch the surface of God's knowledge.

So far we have described God as an eternal, almighty being who is everywhere, knows all, and never changes. This gives us a sense of some of this awesome God's infinite characteristics, but it doesn't get at his personal side or the core of who he is. It is on this personal level that we can relate more to him.

GOD'S RELATIONAL HEART

This infinite God spoke the words, "Let there be..." and the world was created (Genesis 1:3). And he saw that it was good. But when he created, he didn't do it alone, because all three persons of the Godhead were there. "The Spirit of God was hovering over the surface of the water" (Genesis 1:2). The Son, Jesus, was there too. "Christ is the visible image of the invisible God. He existed before anything was created and is supreme over all creation, for through him God created everything" (Colossians 1:15-16). This triune aspect of God demonstrates that he is relational. So before there were humans, before Planet Earth or the universe or time as we know it, he existed eternally as a relational being.

Moses recorded in Scripture that this eternal Creator is the "God who is passionate about his relationship with you" (Exodus 34:14 NLT). And to further define the nature of this relationship the Scripture says that "love comes from God...for God is love" (1 John 4:7-8). We then can say that *God exists as a loving relational being.*

Part of the very reason God created humans was to have a relationship with them.* He didn't do this because he needed a relationship; he already existed as relationship. He created us as relational beings because at his very heart he is a loving relational being who wants to relate to us. Creation was entirely because of his relational goodness and grace.

King David describes the loving heart of God:

> The LORD is compassionate and merciful, slow to get angry and filled with unfailing love (Psalm 103:8).

> Your faithfulness extends to every generation...LORD, how great is your mercy (Psalm 119:90,156).

> He gives justice to the oppressed and food to the hungry. The LORD frees the prisoners. The LORD opens the eyes of the blind. The LORD lifts up those who are weighed down. The LORD loves the godly. The LORD protects the foreigners among us. He cares for the orphans and widows, but he frustrates the plans of the wicked (Psalm 146:7-9).

> He heals the brokenhearted and bandages their wounds (Psalm 147:3).

Do you get the picture? God's relational heart is other-focused. It is

---

* See "Why Did God Create Humans?" on page 58.

compassionate, merciful, unfailing, faithful, just, and caring. His pure heart protects the ones he loves and provides for their good. He makes the security, happiness, and welfare of another as important as his own. His love is giving and trusting, unselfish and sacrificial, secure and safe, loyal and forever.

And when humans didn't believe their loving God had their best interest at heart and rebelled against him, what did he do? Instead of leaving them alone, separated from him in their sin, he reached out in love to draw them back to him.

> God is so rich in mercy, and he loved us so much, that even though we were dead because of our sins, he gave us life when he raised Christ from the dead (Ephesians 2:4-5).

The cost, of course, was the torturous death of His Son on a cruel cross. The innocent and holy Son was willing to suffer and die so that he could restore a relationship with you and me. That is the relational heart of God.

GOD'S HOLY NATURE

It is impossible to grasp or express God's infinite characteristics. We cannot fathom his relational heart of love. Yet he has created us as relational beings, and while we by no means comprehend him exhaustively, we are powerfully drawn to him and can relate to him truly. We were created to love him back and love others as we love ourselves. But where we as humans fail to love perfectly, God does not. For *the infinite God of relationship is holy, perfect, and righteous.* Scripture says, "He is the Rock; his deeds are perfect. Everything he does is just and fair. He is a faithful God who does no wrong; how just and upright he is!" (Deuteronomy 32:4).

Scripture reveals a God who is perfectly holy (Isaiah 54:5 and Revelation 4:8), just (Revelation 16:5), and right (Psalm 119:137). This isn't something he *decides* to do. In other words, he doesn't simply decide to do holy, just, and right things; this is something he *is*. All that is right and holy, just and good is derived from his core nature. The Scripture says, "Whatever is good and perfect comes down to us from God our Father, who created all the lights in the heavens" (James 1:17).

This is incredibly important! What people miss and fail to understand about God is that he is pure goodness. All that is perfect and right and beautiful and complete and meaningful and eternally full of contentment, joy, and happiness is because of him and comes from him. His very nature and essence are good. "The LORD is good and does what is right" (Psalm 25:8). He is "the one who is holy and true" (Revelation 3:7). "Holy, holy, holy is the LORD Almighty" (Isaiah 6:3 NIV). "The LORD is righteous in everything he does; he is filled with kindness" (Psalm 145:17). "The LORD is just! He is my rock! There is no evil in him" (Psalm 92:15).

The unchanging nature of a holy God (his immutability) makes it impossible for him to lie or go against his perfect goodness (Romans 3:3-4 and Hebrews 6:16-18). He then is our absolute standard for defining what is right and wrong, what is good and evil, and what is pure joy and happiness. To live and be godlike is to ultimately experience the rightness, goodness, and joy that he has to offer. To live and be anything else is to ultimately experience evil, suffering, and the absence of all that is good.

If we are to begin to understand who God really is, we must acknowledge that he is the infinite one and be in awe of him, acknowledge his relational nature and embrace him, and acknowledge his pure goodness and worship him. King Solomon said in his wisdom, "The fear of the LORD is the foundation of wisdom. Knowledge of the Holy One results in good judgment" (Proverbs 9:10).

Possessing wisdom and understanding about God, the Bible, and life itself is wrapped up in a knowledge of his infinite characteristics, his relational heart of love, and his nature of pure goodness. With this as our center of moral gravity, we can begin to see life clearly and have a reference point for making right moral choices.

12.

WHO IS THE HOLY SPIRIT?

When we think of God, we may imagine the powerful Creator sitting on his throne in heaven. We may think of him in human form as Jesus, the Savior of the World. But do we view him as the Holy Spirit? Just who is God in the person of the Holy Spirit?

Some people believe the Holy Spirit is simply the influence of good—like the "good force" of the universe. But the Holy Spirit is actually a person—the third person of the Trinity (God the Father, God the Son, and God the Holy Spirit). Jesus referred to the Spirit as a person when he said, "I will ask the Father, and he will give you another Advocate, who will never leave you. He is the Holy Spirit, who leads into all truth" (John 14:16-17).

The Holy Spirit is one of the three persons of God. He has a mind and feelings. He makes choices. Scripture says, "He who searches our hearts knows the mind of the Spirit" (Romans 8:27 NIV). Scripture also tells us that the Spirit can feel. We are not to "bring sorrow to God's Holy Spirit by the way you live" (Ephesians 4:30). He makes choices as to who will receive what spiritual gifts. "It is the one and only Spirit who distributes these gifts" (1 Corinthians 12:11). Also, the apostle Peter told a man named Ananias, "You lied to the Holy Spirit" (Acts 5:3). Ananias wasn't lying to an influence; he was lying to a person. Peter added, "You weren't lying to us but to God" (Acts 5:4).

When God sent the Holy Spirit, he became the interactive agent of God to us. When he was "poured out" on God's people on the Day of Pentecost (see Acts 2) we might say the word "God" was not only a noun—it also became a verb. Rather than just learning who God is or following the teaching of Jesus impersonally, we experience God actually brought into our lives by the Spirit. He is the active, moving God who impels us to action. God the Holy Spirit is about living, loving, responding, enjoying, embracing, comforting, supporting, accepting, encouraging, respecting, disciplining, growing, empowering, and a myriad of other such verbs.

The Holy Spirit is the dynamic, active, and ever-present person of God. We experience him in our everyday living. Further, he demonstrates himself in our capacity to love as God loves. "If we love each other," John said, "God lives in us, and his love has been brought to full expression in us. And God has given us his Spirit as proof that we live in him and he in us" (1 John 4:12-13). The Holy Spirit is real. He evidenced himself powerfully on the Day of Pentecost two millennia ago. And his presence is additional proof that we belong to God, for the "Holy Spirit speaks to us deep in our hearts and tells us that we are God's children" (Romans 8:16 NLT).

13.

WHAT DOES IT MEAN THAT GOD IS A TRINITY?

The idea that God is three in one has confused many people. Just what does it mean that God is a Trinity?

The Bible teaches there is but one God. This is called *monotheism.* "Hear, O Israel: The LORD our God, the LORD is one" (Deuteronomy 6:4 NIV). Jesus quoted this scripture in Mark 12:29, confirming that there is just one God. So how is it that people call God a Trinity—how, some people ask, can there be three Gods, yet one?

God being a Trinity does not mean there are three Gods. God exists as three persons, yet he is one being. Each *person* of the Trinity—the Father, the Son, and the Holy Spirit—has a separate identity while yet possessing the full nature of God.

Jesus is the divine Son of God. This does not mean that Jesus was created by God. In fact, Scripture tells us plainly that he has always co-existed with God (see John 1:1-3). Jesus himself declared he had eternally co-existed with his Father. And on the basis of that declaration the Jewish leaders plotted to kill him, saying, "He called God his Father, thereby making himself equal with God" (John 5:18). Paul the apostle declared Jesus to be deity. "Christ himself was an Israelite as far as his human nature is concerned. And he is God, the one who rules over everything and is worthy of eternal praise!" (Romans 9:5). The writer of Hebrews says, "The Son radiates God's own glory and expresses the very character of God" (Hebrews 1:3).

Therefore, God the Father co-exists with God the Son:

> Christ is the visible image of the invisible God. He existed before God made anything at all and is supreme over all creation. Christ is the one through whom God created everything in heaven and earth…He existed before everything else began, and he holds all creation together (Colossians 1:15-17 NLT).

Paul refers to both the Father and Jesus as God. "It is by the command of God our Savior that I have been entrusted with this work for him… May God the Father and Christ Jesus our Savior give you grace and peace" (Titus 1:3-4). God the Father is deity. God the Son is deity.

God the Holy Spirit is also deity. The apostle Peter recognized this when he pointed out the wrongdoing of a man in the Jerusalem church (Acts 5:3-4). The Spirit has eternally co-existed with the Father and the Son and was present at creation (see Genesis 1:2). Jesus said of him, "I will ask the Father, and he will give you another Advocate…He is the Holy Spirit, who leads into all truth…When the Father sends the Advocate as my representative—that is, the Holy Spirit—he will teach you everything I have told you" (John 14:16,26). Paul said, "When you believed in Christ, he identified you as his own by giving you the Holy Spirit, whom he promised long ago" (Ephesians 1:13). Jesus called the co-existing Spirit holy because he is the Spirit of the Holy God. He is the third person of the triune Godhead.

In conclusion, the doctrine of the Trinity was formulated in faithfulness to the teachings of the Bible about the nature of God, in an effort to express his truth.*

---

* For more information on the Trinity, see chapter 36 of Josh McDowell and Sean McDowell, *The Unshakable Truth* (Eugene, OR: Harvest House Publishers, 2010). For more about *The Unshakable Truth,* see the back of this book.

14.

IS GOD MALE OR FEMALE?

To ask the question, "Is God male or female?" is somewhat like asking if God is right- or left-handed. Or is his first language English or Spanish? Truth is, he is not confined by our human or material world. He created us in his image, but he is unlike us in many, many ways.

Jesus said, "God is Spirit, so those who worship him must worship in spirit and in truth" (John 4:24). It is true that God took on human form in the person of Jesus, who of course was male, yet God does not exist as a material or physical being. So in that sense he is neither male nor female as we know the human sexes.

At the same time, God has chosen to create and use imagery of himself that is both masculine and feminine. Of course he refers to himself as Father and Jesus as the Son of God, which are both masculine imagery. Yet Jesus spoke of himself in feminine imagery when he said, "How often I have wanted to gather your children together as a hen protects her chicks beneath her wings, but you wouldn't let me" (Matthew 23:37).

Some people have suggested that the natural male to female attraction is rooted in the nature of God. The magnetism of man toward woman and woman toward man originates in the unity and completeness of a God who bears the characteristics of both male and female. This idea suggests that God inherently has the "plus and minus" characteristics of male and female, and when these characteristics are placed separately in each sex, they attract like opposite magnetic poles. That at least is one theory of why males and females are attracted to one another.

However, throughout Scripture God has chosen to primarily characterize himself in masculine terms even though he is neither wholly male nor wholly female. And whether we are born male or female, he refers to those he redeems as his children (Romans 8:14), his bride (Ephesians 5:25-27), his holy temple (Ephesians 2:21-22), joint heirs (Romans 8:17), and a royal priesthood, a holy nation, and his very own possession (1 Peter 2:9).

So while God is neither male nor female, he can relate to us as men and women equally, for he loves us equally and has made provision for all of us to be in relationship with him.

15.

CAN GOD DO WRONG, SUCH AS GET JEALOUS?

The Bible says God is a jealous God. But getting jealous is wrong. So how can that be if God doesn't do anything wrong?

If God is anything, he is perfectly good. "He is the Rock; his deeds are perfect," the Scripture states. "Everything he does is just and fair. He is a faithful God who does no wrong; how just and upright he is!" (Deuteronomy 32:4). Additionally, the writer of the book of Hebrews tells us God bound himself with an oath when he made a promise to Abraham, and these two things are based on his sinless character that is unchanging. "God has given both his promise and his oath. These two things are unchangeable because it is impossible for God to lie" (Hebrews 6:18). For God to do wrong would go against his very nature and character, which he cannot do.*

HOW CAN GOD'S JEALOUSY BE OKAY?

But if God can do no wrong, then why does the Bible say he gets jealous? Certainly being jealous is wrong—at least we as humans are not to get jealous. Right?

In 1 Corinthians Paul says, "You are still controlled by your sinful nature. You are jealous of one another and quarrel with each other" (1 Corinthians 3:3). It is clearly wrong to be selfishly possessive and contentious toward those who have something you want, and the apostle was pointing this out. Yet in the very next letter he wrote to the Corinthians he said, "I am jealous for you with the jealousy of God himself" (2 Corinthians 11:2). Here Paul is concerned that their "pure and undivided devotion to Christ will be corrupted" (verse 2) and so he was jealous like God is jealous. Obviously, Paul isn't condemning the jealousy of God. So what kind of jealousy does God display?

In Exodus it says, "You must worship no other gods, for the LORD, whose very name is Jealous, is a God who is jealous about his relationship

---

* For more on God's pure character see the answer to "What Is God Really Like?" on page 39.

with you" (Exodus 34:14). Joshua also told the children of Israel that their God was "a holy and jealous God" (Joshua 24:19). These two words "jealous God" in the Hebrew are *el qana,* which denotes passion and zeal. Although the word *jealous* in English is mostly used in an evil sense, in the Hebrew it expresses passion and caring, most often in connection with the marriage relationship. God considered the children of Israel as his marriage partner, and he wanted them to love him as a wife would devote herself exclusively to her husband. That is why he said they were to worship no other but him. He wants to be loved with a pure and passionate love reserved only for him.

A HUMAN EXAMPLE

As relational beings we can relate to wanting to be loved exclusively. How would you feel if someone said that he or she truly loves you and then cheated on you? It's not wrong to feel bad about someone cheating on you, is it? Isn't it natural to want to be number one in someone's life?

Imagine me (Sean) being on my honeymoon. As Stephanie and I are strolling romantically along on a beach I turn to her, look deeply into her eyes, and say, "Stephanie honey, of all the more than three billion women on this planet, you are on my top-10 list." You watch as my new wife leans her head on my shoulder and gazes into my eyes. "Gee, Sean, thanks. That means so much. It thrills me to think that I'm among the ten women you love! Just to be on your list, sweetheart, is good enough for me."

Can you imagine that kind of a response? I can't. Stephanie would be insulted, hurt, and upset if I loved even one other woman besides her. And she should be. My wife wants to be number one in my life. And I want to be considered the number-one man in her life. You and I were relationally created that way. We are designed to jealously want each other's exclusive love.

And because God is perfectly good and holy, his jealousy is not in any way selfish. He knows that when we love him exclusively—with all our heart, soul, and strength—it allows us to experience the joy and meaning we are looking for in life. That is the reason he calls us to worship him and him only. It is by no means wrong for God to jealously want our exclusive love and devotion. In fact, his jealous love is a model for us to follow.

16

WHERE DID EVIL COME FROM?

Evil had to come from somewhere, right? But from where? Scripture states that God "is a faithful God who does no wrong; how just and upright he is!" (Deuteronomy 32:4). And yet it states that God "created everything there is. Nothing exists that he didn't make" (John 1:3 NLT). So if the Creator of all things is good with no evil, how is it that evil is in the world? We know that evil exists and that God made everything, so how can we say that God didn't create evil? And if he didn't create it, where did it come from?

God is perfectly good and holy and created only perfect creatures. Yet he gave his human creation the power of free choice or free will. The first humans had a choice to trust in him, to believe that he was good and that he had their best interest at heart when he gave them a command to obey. Unfortunately they used this good power to choose against him, and that brought evil into this world.

EVIL'S POSSIBILITY

So the possibility of evil did arise from God, but not directly. Evil came from an abuse of a good power called free will. God may be responsible for the possibility of evil existing in the world, yet it was the choice of humans that made evil a reality in the world. We can say that God produces the *fact* of free choice, but it is the individual man or woman who performs the *act* of free choice.

Of course God could have created a world without free will. Humans could have been "programmed" to do good and worship him perfectly. Yet in a world without choices the true meaning of "I love you" would be lost. The fulfilling purpose and reality of loving another is void and meaningless without the power to freely choose. God wanted us to experience the reality of a love relationship together with him. The great risk was the possibility of evil. And the great responsibility to act on that possibility rested with humans, not God.

EVIL'S ACTUALITY

So God made evil possible, yet humans made it actual. But what was it that caused the first humans to choose evil?* In the case of Eve, the first woman, she made a choice to eat a fruit that God had commanded her and her husband, Adam, not to eat. The first couple had the power of free will. They could have chosen to obey God and not eat of the forbidden fruit. But when the serpent—the tempter—told Eve, in effect, that God didn't know what he was talking about, she listened. The serpent said she would become like God, knowing everything, both good and evil. The Scripture says, "The woman was convinced. She saw that the tree was beautiful and its fruit looked delicious, and she wanted the wisdom it would give her. So [by the act of her free will] she took some of the fruit and ate it" (Genesis 3:6).

Eve had been given a good thing by God. She was given the power to choose between *her* determining what *she* considered right and wrong versus allowing him to be the sole arbiter of what was right and wrong. God was, and is, the Sovereign who decides right from wrong. Yet Eve wanted that prerogative—she wanted to be self-sovereign, with the ability to choose for herself what she thought was in her best interest.

So to summarize: Where did evil come from, and what caused the first human to choose it? Eve coveted God's wisdom—his sovereign determination of what was in the best interest of humans. He gave the first couple the power of free will, and they chose to follow their own desires rather than his. Evil was born out of a choice to believe that God was denying his human creation what was good. As a result, the first humans committed an evil act of self-sovereignty in disobedience to their Creator's command.

---

* See "What Causes People to Sin Today?" on page 54.

17.

WHAT IS EVIL EXACTLY?

Human beings first experienced evil when the original couple exercised the power of free will and chose to distrust God and go against him.* Since we know evil exists, what is it exactly? Is evil an entity, a thing that exists in and of itself, outside of the free will of a human being?

Scripture clearly states that God created everything (see John 1:1-3 and Colossians 1:15-17). And if we accept that evil is a reality, how can we say he didn't create it? The answer lies in the fact that evil is not a thing or substance or entity to be created. Rather, evil is the corruption of a good thing that God did in fact make. Let's explain.

God made humans and it was good. This is repeated multiple times in Genesis 1. He gave humans the power of free will, and that was good as well. This means he gave them the choice to believe he was the arbiter of right and wrong and that he knew what was best for them when he said not to eat of a certain fruit—and that was good. When the first humans believed he did *not* know what was best for them—which was the corrupting of a particular good thing—evil was then born.

Evil then is not a substance or an entity, but the corruption of that which is good. This means that evil is parasitic upon good. In other words, evil depends upon the existence of good in a way good does not depend upon evil. Thus, while there can be good without evil, there cannot be evil without the existence of goodness. Just as the concept of "bentness" requires "straightness," the existence of evil requires that good be previously in existence.

Evil became a reality when there was 1) a rejection of what God said was true and worthy of obedience, and 2) an act in opposition to his command. He wanted humans to trust and obey him. In fact, he designed all of us to live fulfilled and meaningful lives by worshipping him and living in right relationship with him. And when the choice was made to cease trusting in him and following his ways, evil became a reality.

---

* See "Where Did Evil Come From?" on page 51.

18.

WHAT CAUSES PEOPLE TO SIN TODAY?

You have probably heard someone who has done something wrong offer this as a reason for their action: "The devil made me do it." Does Satan, people, or temptation make us do wrong? What is it that causes people to sin? And by sin, we mean any thought, attitude, or action that does not express or conform to the holy character and nature of God.*

THE HUMAN CONDITION

To understand the *cause* of people's sinning, we need to understand the *condition* of people who sin. And we need not look any further than ourselves or our own children for that understanding. If you have been around children very long, you can testify that a child without any training has an independent streak that is "me-centered." From infancy, it appears, we struggle for control to get what we want when we want it and in the way we want it. In one form or another this independent drive to be in charge lies behind every struggle for power, every prejudice, every conflict, and every abuse of relationship since the dawn of time. This propensity to sin comes from within each of us. But we might ask, "Where did this compulsion to do wrong come from?"

When the first couple, Adam and Eve, was confronted with a choice, they were living in a perfect world in perfect relationship with God. But because he had given them free will—the power to choose—the possibility for evil existed.† They could have believed that God's command not to eat from the tree of the knowledge of good and evil was an unselfish prohibition and that he had their best interest at heart. But they did not.

"When Adam sinned," the Scripture says, "sin entered the world. Adam's sin brought death, so death spread to everyone, for everyone sinned" (Romans 5:12). This means we start off from birth with a self-centered, self-serving nature that wants what we want when we want it. So it's not the devil that makes us sin or anyone else. Evil isn't an entity outside us luring us to sin. The sinful nature within us is a result of being

---

* See "What Is God Really Like?" on page 39.

† See "Where Did Evil Come From?" on page 51.

spiritually separated from an intimate and unbroken relationship with a holy God. And it is this sinful nature that has a "craving for physical pleasure, a craving for everything we see, and the pride in our achievements and possessions" (1 John 2:16). "For wherever there is jealousy and sinful ambition, there you will find disorder and evil of every kind" (James 3:16).

IT'S NOT THAT BAD, IS IT?

Sin is the depraved condition of the entire human race. Yet we often prefer to think that our sin disposition isn't all that bad. But the depravity of humans runs to the very core and gives them the capacity for cruelty and heartless acts against the innocent. For example, from 1932 to 1933 millions of Ukrainian citizens were forced to die of starvation for political reasons. There were the death camps of Dachau, Buchenwald, and Auschwitz, where millions of Jewish men, women, and children were gassed by the Nazis during World War II. Others at that time faced the demented medical experiments of Josef Mengele, who put men, women, and children through torturous procedures for the "advancement of the Aryan race."

Historically, the brutality of war has included horrific torture of every kind, wholesale rape, and mass starvation. The media chronicled the acts of "ethnic cleansing" in Croatia and Bosnia and Herzegovina during the 1980s and 1990s. Awareness of the ongoing horrors in Sudan and Darfur continues to rise. Human evil is as recent as today's news. As of this writing we learned that "a U.N. investigation concluded Monday that Syrian forces committed crimes against humanity by killing and torturing hundreds of children, including a 2-year-old girl reportedly shot to death so she wouldn't grow up to be a demonstrator."[9] For centuries the world has witnessed the barbaric mistreatment of humans by humans.

We say these terrible acts are inhumane and inhuman. But the reality is that they are thoroughly human—the result of people's depraved nature. The human race has an unimaginable capacity for evil. In each of our hearts are the seeds of cruelty and corruption. Scripture says, "All have become corrupt. No one does good, not a single one!" (Psalm 14:3). The cause of sin is from within, not from outside forces.

The good news, however, is that God sent his only Son to forgive us of our sins and purify our hearts. Jesus said, "Blessed are the pure in heart, for they shall see God" (Matthew 5:8 NASB).

19.

IF GOD IS SO LOVING, WHY CAN'T HE BE MORE TOLERANT OF SIN?

We all know that God has a serious problem with sin, but why can't he be less demanding and more understanding of our imperfections? We may think something like *Why can't God just be more forgiving and overlook our weaknesses and failures?* If he is truly loving he should be more tolerant of our shortcomings, right?

The reality is that God is merciful, but that isn't quite the same as being tolerant. First, many people fail to understand the seriousness of sin and the great cost to God personally to forgive us our sins. When we see the combination of his holiness and justice we gain a greater understanding of his mercy. And that will go a long way to answering why he can't tolerate sin and yet can be merciful at the same time.

There is a reason God can't stand sin. You see, his core nature is holy and pure. There is no impurity of motive or action with him, for he is perfect and without sin. (See Deuteronomy 32:4; Isaiah 54:5; and Revelation 4:8.) So a holy God cannot be in relationship with sin in any manner. The Bible says of him, "Your eyes are too pure to look on evil; you cannot tolerate wrong" (Habakkuk 1:13 NIV). He is so holy that he "cannot allow sin in any form" (Habakkuk 1:13). To do so would violate the very essence of who he is.

THE SEPARATION

So our sin naturally separates us from God. And a relational separation from him causes spiritual death. The "wages of sin," the Bible says, "is death" (Romans 6:23). It is this death or separation from God that preserves his holiness.

And yet because he is a God of love, the Bible declares of him that "you...delight to show mercy" (Micah 7:18 NIV). King David said that his "mercy endures forever" (Psalm 107:1 NKJV). In the New Testament it says, "God is so rich in mercy, and he loved us so much" (Ephesians 2:4). But even with God being merciful toward us, there is the problem we mentioned—the problem with sin. God can't have any relationship with sin, and we as humans have a condition called sin. So what is he to do?

HOW GOD'S CHARACTERISTICS COMBINE

The answer lies in the combination of his loving mercy and his perfect justice. Mercy in and of itself cannot overlook or even forgive sin without sin being dealt with justly. Sin has to be paid for. And that is where God's justice comes in.

"The LORD is just!" the Bible says. "He is my rock! There is no evil in him!" (Psalm 92:15). "All his acts are just and true" (Daniel 4:37). It is his just nature that demands that sin be separated from purity, that wrong be righted, and evil be vanquished. Yet in this righteous insistence upon justice, he is still merciful. "We cannot imagine the power of the Almighty; but even though he is just and righteous, he does not destroy us" (Job 37:23). So instead of being tolerant of our sin, God's sense of justice combined with mercy makes the payment for it.

So in his mercy he pays for our sin with nothing less than the life of his only Son. We inherited our sin condition at birth from the first human couple that sinned (Romans 5:12). But "God paid a ransom to save you from the empty life you inherited from your ancestors. The ransom he paid was not mere gold or silver. It was the precious blood of Christ, the sinless, spotless Lamb of God" (1 Peter 1:18-19).

The "spotless Lamb of God" satisfies the demand of both God's holiness and his justice. His holiness is satisfied because Jesus was sinless—a perfect sacrifice without sin. We are "justified freely by his grace through the redemption that came by Christ Jesus. God presented him as a sacrifice of atonement, through faith in his blood" (Romans 3:24-25 NIV). His justice is satisfied because Christ's death paid our "wages of sin," which is death. God paid a very high price to grant us forgiveness. While he cannot be tolerant of sin, he has paid the price so he can extend his mercy to us through Christ.

20.

WHY DID GOD CREATE HUMANS?

Was God lonely and wanted someone to relate to…so he made humans? Was he bored and one day got really creative and produced a universe that included people? Just why did he create human beings?

After God created the first human he made a startling declaration, "It is not good…" (Genesis 2:18). He had created everything before this, and after each stage of creation he "saw that it was good." Yet in this perfect world, before humans sinned, God stated something wasn't good. What was this "not good" thing? It was man's aloneness.

Some people have speculated as follows: Since aloneness was not good even in a perfect world, God must have felt alone too and that is the reason he created humans. Perhaps he wanted or needed a human relationship, so he created human beings to remove his own aloneness. One big problem with this thinking is that it implies something is *lacking* in God. And yet if he is perfect, nothing can be lacking.

The other problem with this notion is that the eternal God never has been alone. Consisting as he does of three persons, he has existed eternally as relationship. A continuous cycle of perfect relationships has been eternally experienced within the Godhead of the Father, the Son, and the Holy Spirit.*

It's true the first human was created alone. But God remedied the "not good" by creating another human for the purpose of human relationships. So then, why did God create humans in the first place if he wasn't lonely?

THE JOY OF RELATIONSHIP

When God said, "Let us make human beings in our image, to be like ourselves" (Genesis 1:26), he was designing each of us to live and enjoy life in relationship as he did. While we can never comprehend the perfect

---

* See "What Does It Mean that God Is a Trinity?" on page 46.

relationship within the Trinity in an absolute sense, we do have the capacity to experience the joy of what relationships truly offer.

Jesus said, "I have told you this so that my joy may be in you and that your joy may be complete" (John 15:11 NIV). God in effect is saying, "Become intimate with me, allow my joy to be in you, and through our close relationship you will experience the true joy of living, for you will bear the fruit of my nature—love, joy, peace, patience, kindness, goodness, faithfulness, gentleness, and self-control (see Galatians 5:22-23). And in doing so you will reflect my presence and give me glory!" *And that is why God created humans—to give himself glory.*

In 1647 the English Reformers created the Westminster Catechism, which included 107 questions and answers. The first was, "What is the chief end of man?" The answer: "Man's chief end is to glorify God, and to enjoy him forever." That states the reason God created humans very succinctly.

"Everything comes from him," Scripture states, "and exists by his power and is intended for his glory" (Romans 11:36). "Give to the LORD the glory he deserves!" (1 Chronicles 16:29). No matter what is said or thought or done, the Bible admonishes us to "do it all for the glory of God" (1 Corinthians 10:31), "so that in all things God may be glorified" (1 Peter 4:11 NASB).

To bring glory to God—that is, to exalt him, lift him up, give him praise, to reflect upon him honorably—is in fact our purpose in life. Even though sin broke our relationship with him, because of Christ our godlikeness can be restored, as "we who with unveiled faces all reflect the Lord's glory, are being transformed into his likeness with ever-increasing glory, which comes from the Lord, who is the Spirit" (2 Corinthians 3:18 NIV). So God created us so we could eternally enjoy a relationship with him, and in doing so bring great honor and glory to him.

21.

DID GOD CREATE INTELLIGENT BEINGS OTHER THAN HUMANS?

Are we the only finite intelligent beings in the universe? Are there others out there somewhere that God created who are our "alien relatives"? Many have speculated that intelligent life exists somewhere in the distant universe—it's just that we haven't made contact with it yet.

King David wrote, "When I look at the night sky and see the work of your fingers—the moon and the stars you set in place—what are mere mortals that you should think about human beings that you should care for them?" (Psalm 8:3-4). The space that God created, in its vastness and wonder, is majestic and awesome and beyond our comprehension.

Scientists say matter is spread over a space at least 93 billion light-years across. There are probably more than 100 billion galaxies in the observable universe, with countless billions of planets.[10] That blows the mind! And it may cause us to wonder, are we the only intelligent beings God created in this vast universe?

There have been many books and studies and reports that claim to have credible evidence substantiating the existence of extraterrestrial beings. And there have been just as many books and reports to refute and counter those claims. One thing seems certain—if there were extraterrestrials capable of visiting earth, they haven't elected to make their presence known widely to the public.

Nothing in Scripture reveals that there is intelligent life on other planets. Scripture is silent on this issue. We are told there are demons, angels, seraphim, and cherubim, but there is no reference to other intelligent life.

But if there was life on other distant planets, it would not seem to contradict Christian beliefs. God is the creator of the universe, and if he created other life-forms and didn't tell us about it—that's his prerogative. And just because he chooses not to tell us doesn't necessarily mean there aren't other intelligent beings out there. The point is, we simply don't know.

22.

IS IT REALLY EVEN POSSIBLE
TO KNOW TRUTH?

So far throughout this book we have attempted to answer 21 questions. And many of the questions assume truths exist about God and Scripture—truths that provide satisfying answers. In other words, if we discover certain truths we gain knowledge about or answers to our questions. But are there actually universal truths that can answer these questions...or does it really come down to what we subjectively choose to believe? In other words, is there a way to really know that there is a truth that is universally true?

SOME DEFINITIONS

First, let's start by defining *truth*. What do we mean when we say *truth*? Typically, two definitions are offered to explain the same concept of truth. Webster defines truth, in part, as "fidelity to an original or standard." For example, say I (Sean) asked you, "What time is it?" You would probably look at your watch or cell phone and say something like, "It's 2:23 p.m." But what if I look at my watch and say, "No, it's 2:26 p.m." Whose statement is the truth, yours or mine?

We could argue all day about whose device is the better timepiece. But to determine the correct time we would have to measure our watches against the international standard where all time is measured. That would be Greenwich, England. That is home to Greenwich Mean Time (GMT). GMT is *world time* and is the basis of every world time zone. Although GMT has been replaced by *atomic time* (UTC), it is still widely regarded as the official measurement of time around the globe.

So to establish which "truth statement" is in fact true—your 2:23 p.m. or my 2:26 p.m., we would simply measure them against the "original or standard" of time-keeping in Greenwich. The time that is in accord with GMT is the correct time. Applying that same truth definition to moral truth, we assert that God is the absolute standard for all moral truth. It is his very nature and character that define what is right and wrong, good and evil, and true and untrue.

The second definition of truth is "that which corresponds to reality." This is roughly the idea that a truth statement is true if it matches up with the way the real world actually is. For example, I (Josh) might say that Dottie and I have four grown children, two boys and two girls. The question is, "Is that statement true or false?" The statement can be proven true if it matches up with reality. And in reality I have four children, three girls and one boy. So since my statement didn't fit reality, my statement would not be true. And when we apply this definition of truth to moral truth, we assert that moral truth conforms to the reality that God has created.

DENYING TRUTH'S EXISTENCE

But some people say simply, "There is no truth." The problem with this phrase is that it is *self-contradictory*. In other words, the sentence refutes itself through its very existence. Let me (Sean) explain. At the commencement of his letter to Titus, Paul gives some advice to Titus, who is starting churches among the Cretan people. He is being confronted with some hostile ideas. Paul quotes Epimenides, a Cretan, saying to Titus, "Even one of their own prophets has said, 'Cretans are always liars, evil brutes, lazy gluttons'" (Titus 1:12 NIV). Any astute Bible reader would catch the irony in this statement. If *all* Cretans are liars, then how can Epimenides himself really be trusted? It would be like me, as a Californian, saying, "You can't trust anybody from California."

The statements "Cretans are always liars" and "there is no truth" suffer from the same defect: *Both statements contradict themselves.* The statement "there is no truth" is a truth claim about at least one thing—namely, that "there is no truth." Yet this statement contradicts itself by claiming that truth does not exist. Here are some other examples of self-contradictory statements:

- There are no English sentences with more than five words. (You just gave one!)

- There is no such thing as absolute truth. (Is that absolutely true?)

- We cannot be sure about anything. (Are you sure about that?)

- Never say the word "never." (Too late—you've already said it!)

All four of these statements—like the phrase "there is no truth"—contain the seeds of their own destruction. They undermine themselves by contradicting their own standard for truth. There is no way to escape the fact that truth exists and that it can be known. Thus, the most important question becomes not if we can know truth, but what *is* truth?

Jesus made it clear what truth was when he said, "I am the way, the truth, and the life" (John 14:6). In other words, truth is actually a person we can relate to. God is not only our standard of moral truth, which corresponds to the reality he has created, but he is a person who has gone to extraordinary lengths to form a relationship with us. And relationship is key in knowing and living out the truth.

23.

IS SOME TRUTH JUST PERSONAL PREFERENCE?

You have probably heard someone say, "Well, that may be true for you, but it's not true for me." Although this is a commonly used phrase, we must ask, can truth exist solely for the person who believes it? Can something be true for one person but not another?

CLEARING UP CONFUSION

Behind the above phrase lies a deep-seated confusion between the concepts of *truth* and *belief*. Clearly, we are each entitled to our own beliefs (at least in America, the land of the free), but does this mean that we each have our own respective truths? Truth is independent of our beliefs. Beliefs, on the other hand, are necessarily personal. Therefore, when we consider the nature of truth it makes no sense to say that something is true for you and not for me.

For example, imagine that you and your friend encounter a green apple lying on a table. Your friend believes the inside is rotten and full of worms. But you, on the other hand, believe it is crisp and worm-free. Can your varying beliefs about the apple create two distinct truths that each of you experience as reality? The only way to solve the dilemma is to slice open the apple and observe its insides. Then you will be in a position to discover the truth about the apple—if it has worms or not. The instant the apple is sliced the truth will be revealed and the false beliefs will be exposed. The truth about the apple exists independently of you and your friend's beliefs about it.

MORAL TRUTHS AND BELIEFS

This is the same when it comes to moral truths. God and his Word become the standard of what is morally true or not because moral truths stem from his character.* So while moral truths are not up for consider-

---

* See "Is It Really Even Possible to Know Truth?" on page 61.

ation as personal or subjective, beliefs can be. Personal beliefs can also be considered what some people call "personal convictions." In the book of Romans the apostle Paul was addressing the fact that some Jewish followers of Christ were conflicted over what eating restrictions to follow and what festival days to observe and what day to celebrate the Sabbath. He told them that "those who don't eat certain foods must not condemn those who do, for God has accepted them" (Romans 14:3). And on what day to worship he said, "You should each be fully convinced that whichever day you choose is acceptable" (Romans 14:5).

Paul was making the point that there were issues outside of the universal moral law of God that required a personal decision and were between that person and God. I (Sean) know some people who feel very strongly that to honor the Lord's Day they must refrain from buying products on Sunday. Some people feel it is right to place their children in Christian schools and it would be wrong for them to enroll their kids in public school. Many of these people don't condemn those who do otherwise, but they feel these are personal convictions or beliefs they must follow. The apostle Paul made this point quite clear when he referred to the Jewish regulations on what foods were pure or impure. "I know and am convinced," Paul said, "on the authority of the Lord Jesus that no food, in and of itself, is wrong to eat. But if someone believes it is wrong [for them], then for that person it is wrong" (Romans 14:14).

The primary point Paul was making was that when someone has a personal conviction on issues not clearly addressed in the moral law, he or she should not condemn others for violating his or her particular belief. These types of personal convictions are developed between God and the individual and are not to be imposed upon others. Personal conviction should be arrived at after great care, study of Scripture, and the wise counsel of other mature Christians.

24

IS GOD SEXIST?

As Christians we view God through a completely different set of lenses than atheists, non-Christians, and the cultures of the world. But as you may know, God has been portrayed in many distorted ways. For example, he is said to be misogynic (woman-hating), chauvinistic, patriarchal, and sexist— along with having many other derogatory characteristics—by modern-day atheists and many others. Atheist Richard Dawkins has stated in his book *The God Delusion* that

> the God of the Old Testament is arguably the most unpleasant character in all fiction: jealous and proud of it; a petty, unjust, unforgiving control freak; a vindictive, bloodthirsty ethnic cleanser; a misogynistic, homophobic, racist, infanticidal, genocidal, filicidal, pestilential, megalomaniacal, sadomasochistic, capriciously malevolent bully.[11]

How is it that some can say God is sexist, racist, vindictive, genocidal, and so on? To get these distorted views of him, one has to take Scripture completely out of context. Take the accusation of sexism, for example. How can a person consider God a sexist?

Well, it is said that God created Adam first and then created Eve as a second-class citizen thereby showing his lesser view of women. Then after Adam and Eve sinned, God told Eve that her husband "will rule over you" (Genesis 3:16). Again, this is said to show his disdaining view of women as inferior, in that he said they would be in a submissive, servant role to men. Then some people say one can see all throughout the Old Testament how the children of Israel's customs and laws reflected women's inferior position to men.

For example, an adult woman was considered a minor by law and lived under the authority of her nearest male relative. Her vows to God could even be nullified by her father or husband (Numbers 30:3-16). A husband could divorce his wife (Deuteronomy 24:1-4) and take another wife (Exodus 21:10; Deuteronomy 21:15-17). Yet the wife could not divorce her husband. A woman could inherit her father's land only if there were no male heirs, and only if she married within her ancestral tribe (Numbers 27:1-11; 36:1-13). All these points are again said to show that God viewed women as inferior and without the same rights as men.

HOW GOD ACTUALLY VIEWS MEN AND WOMEN

The truth is that despite these assertions, *God is not a sexist.* This is not to say that historically the church has not treated women as inferior or that some Christian men have not in fact been sexists. It's clear sexist behavior has plagued us for centuries. Yet God is not so and does not consider women inferior to men.

"God said, 'Let us make human beings in our image, to be like us… male and female he created them" (Genesis 1:26-27). The woman was made in the same image and likeness of God as the man (in fact, men were made from dust but women from a human being!). Men were not given a more superior image of God, with the Creator somehow making women in a lesser image. Men and women equally share God's image.

The Bible says God made woman as man's "helper." Some have said this proves women are to serve. Yet God was not creating the female as a servant or assistant to the male. The Hebrew word translated "helper" is *ezer.* It denotes one who surrounds, protects, or aids. It is this same word that Jacob used of God when he said, "May the God of your father *help* you" (Genesis 49:25). Moses used it when he said, "The God of my ancestors was my *helper*" (Exodus 18:4). The psalmist David used it repeatedly in passages like, "We put our hope in the LORD. He is our *help* and our shield" (Psalm 33:20). God is primarily portrayed by the Old Testament writers as the *ezer*—the one who surrounds us and helps us.

This by no means is a lowly servant role. Rather, it is a lofty role to bring help to one who needs it. And I (Sean) can personally attest to the reality that this male—me—needs the aid and help of not only God, but the expert aid and help of a woman named Stephanie. When God created a female as a godlike equal to help the male, it was a highly esteemed role, not one of inferiority or servitude. When he decided that the man was in need of a woman, it didn't mean Adam was inferior either. And women are not inferior for being a counterpart or companion to men.

MORE COMPARISONS

The consequences of sin upon Eve are another purported example of God being a sexist. Yet the negative consequences of sin had a far-reaching effect upon *all* humanity and beyond. They include spiritual and physical death for all humans, women's physical pain in childbearing, husbands ruling over wives, and the cursed ground affecting plant life, making it hard for humans to grow crops (see Genesis 3:14-19). But these negative consequences were not meant to be accepted as norms. God himself put a plan in motion even before he created humans to reverse these consequences. He planned to send his Son to not only offer eternal life to humans who were dead in their sin, but to eventually reverse the effects of sin on the entire planet and animal life (see Isaiah 25:7-8 and 65:17).

Think about this: Are we as God's creation to sit still and not assist him in his redemption and restoration plan? Are we not to discover new and improved ways to farm the land and increase crop productivity? Are we to accept pain in childbearing and not find medical means to reduce it? We of course use modern farm technology to grow better and healthier crops. We take advantage of modern medical discoveries to ease the pain of the birthing process. We don't accept these negative consequences of sin and live with them. And neither should we accept the negative consequences of husbands that rule over their wives. This was not God's intention from the beginning, and it is clear he doesn't want that kind of distorted relationship in marriage now.

While the New Testament does say that wives are to submit to their husbands, this is by no means oppressive. In fact, Scripture commands that we all submit to one another (see Ephesians 5:21). Jesus made the truth clear that both men and women are to serve one another in Mark 10:42-44, a statement that included him also: "Even the Son of Man came not to be served but to serve others and give his life as a ransom for many" (Mark 10:45). Just because husbands and wives serve in different roles doesn't mean women are considered inferior. It is true that sin has brought negative consequences to our relationships, but God doesn't want that to continue. He wants both husbands and wives to respect and love one another as he demonstrated to us through Christ.

And finally, throughout Scripture we see that God elevated women to places of authority and godly leadership. A sexist would not do that. In fact, Genesis is the only creation story of the ancient Near East that even mentions women. And it climaxes with the creation of woman. Clearly, God has valued women since the beginning.

MAKING A COMPARISON

But there is more. In the nation of Israel, women were to be present at the reading of Scripture (Deuteronomy 31:9-13), which was highly honored. Women served at the entrance of the Tabernacle (Exodus 38:8), which was an honorable duty, and they offered sacrifices (Leviticus 12:1-8), which demonstrated God's recognition of the right of women to worship. He appointed Miriam, Moses' sister, as a prophet (Exodus 15:20-21). Deborah was both a prophet and a judge. She spoke and judged publically in the name of God (Judges 4:4-7). And Huldah equally was a prophet of God. She too spoke on his behalf (2 Kings 22:14-20). It is clear he did not regard women as inferior and unable to lead and speak for him.

Further, although critics falsely claim that God is sexist, many of these same critics fail to point out that leaders of other major religions were clearly so. In the book *Apologetics for a New Generation,** author and Christian leader Jonalyn Grace Fincher offers insights about this. In chapter 16 she points out that Muhammad, founder of Islam, had a disparaging view of women. She points out that the Qur'an says, "Wives are fields to seed as you please," "(Wives) are prisoners with you (husbands), having no control of their person," and "Put women in an inferior position since God has done so."[12]

Siddhartha Gautama, founder of Buddhism, abandoned his wife, son, and concubines to find "enlightenment." Charles Taze Russell, founder of the Jehovah's Witnesses, reportedly molested his foster child, Rose Ball. When Russell's wife filed for divorce the courts judged his behavior toward his wife as "insulting," "domineering," and "improper."[13]

In contrast, Jesus, the Son of God, affirmed the rights of women when he spoke to the Samaritan woman (John 4:1-42). He affirmed Mary as she sat at his feet as his disciple. He gave great praise to the women who anointed him before his death (Mark 14:3-9). To Jesus, women were equals in God's eyes. Relationally God sees no human status difference between male and female. As we stated, husbands and wives may serve in different roles, but this does not make one more superior or inferior to the other. The apostle Paul made it clear that God did not engage in favoritism when he said,

---

* Harvest House Publishers, 2009. For more information about *Apologetics for a New Generation,* see the back of this book.

You are all children of God through faith in Christ Jesus. And all who have been united with Christ in baptism have put on Christ, like putting on new clothes. There is no longer Jew or Gentile, slave or free, male or female. For you are all one in Christ Jesus (Galatians 3:26-28).

25.

IS GOD RACIST?

A racist is one who believes that a certain human race is superior to any or all others—that one race or some races have distinctive characteristics determined by hereditary factors, and this endows them with an intrinsic superiority. And this means that racial discrimination is justified. So based on this definition, is God a racist? Some say he is.

In the book of Genesis it tells us God singled out a man named Abram and said,

> Leave your native country, your relatives, and your father's family, and go to the land I will show you. I will make into you a great nation. I will bless you and make you famous, and you will be a blessing to others. I will bless those who bless you and curse those who treat you with contempt. All the families on earth will be blessed through you (Genesis 12:1-3).

If you take this promise from God and then examine how he has favored the children of Israel (the Jewish people), some would say there is no doubt that he racially discriminates. All throughout history, as recorded in Scripture, God has had a chosen race. This, some say, is proof he is a racist.

Another example of God's alleged racism is when he, as some say, cursed the African people into slavery. Many people used to claim that God cursed the descendants of Ham, Noah's son, for telling his older brothers that he found his father naked after a night of drinking wine. The curse was that "he be the lowest of servants to his relatives" (Genesis 9:25). And since the descendants of Ham were thought to be Africans, it was logical to conclude that God had discriminated against all generations of Africans, including condemning them to slavery.

CORRECTING MISINTERPRETATIONS

Both of these charges against God come from misinterpreting and misunderstanding the biblical narrative. First, he never cursed Ham for what he had done—it was Noah who spoke the curse. And Noah didn't curse his son Ham, but rather Ham's son Canaan. "May Canaan be cursed!" Noah said. "May the LORD, the God of Shem, be blessed and may Canaan be his servant" (Genesis 9:25-26). It was more drastic to curse a man's son than to curse the father, so Noah leveled his curse at Ham's son Canaan.

It is true that at least two sons of Ham, Cush and Mizraim, settled in Africa (see Genesis 10:6-20). But Canaan's descendants settled just east of the Mediterranean Sea, in a region that later became known as the land of Canaan—present-day Israel (see Genesis 10:15-19). So it is absurd to claim that God is a racist based upon a complete misinterpretation of passages in Genesis. Yet for many years people justified their own racist views toward black Africans and African–Americans upon this twisting of Scripture.

And what about God's view of the Jewish people? It is true that he made a special covenant with Abraham and his descendants, the Jewish people—and for good reason. Before creation, God planned to redeem sinful humans, and he would do that by taking on the form of humanity through the birth of Jesus. So he identified a people. He gave them his holy Word, the Scripture. He established a sacrificial system with them that would lead to a final remedy for sin and death. He prophesied in his Word that the perfect sacrifice—the Lamb of God—would be born out of the descendants of Abraham (see Matthew 1:1-17). And it was the God-man, Jesus, who came to redeem all who would receive him, both Jew and Gentile.

So God's choosing Israel wasn't simply about Israel—it was about his making his name known and offering salvation to the rest of the world. Also, he judged Israel as he did other nations (see 2 Kings 17). He was not playing favorites. Whether Jew or Gentile, we all equally must give an account to God.

26.

IS GOD LEGALISTIC?

A legalist is a person who believes in strict adherence to the law or to a particular code as an end in and of itself. To a legalist, following the law is what it is all about. So is God a legalist?

Many see God's apparent obsession with law-giving as proof of his legalism. And he did hand down a lot of laws and instructions. In the Old Testament there are very specific laws—the moral law, Israel's civil law, the ceremonial or sacrificial laws, purification laws; there are regulations for what to eat, how to dress, when and how to worship, who you can marry and not marry—the laws, instructions, and rules seem to go on and on and on. And with the laws come some harsh punishments for lawbreakers. It would appear on the surface that God is pretty much a legalist.

Those who see God as a legalist, however, miss the reason he gave the law. There is a "heart reason" that motivated God to provide his instruction. He told the children of Israel, "'I know the plans I have for you,' says the LORD. 'They are plans for good and not for disaster, to give you a future and a hope'" (Jeremiah 29:11). God's law—his plans—were there to make Israel prosper. They were for their good.

The two loving motivations God has in giving us his law are to provide for us and to protect us. It is a relational reason. Truth is, he wants us to follow his instructions because they represent his ways—ways that provide for us, protect us, and bring us joy. So each time we are obedient to his law we are in effect acting according to his ways.

What many people seem to miss is that God's ways reflect who he is. And when we begin to act in a godlike manner, we live as we were meant to live. You see, God by his very nature and character defines all that is perfect, right, good—those things that bring us true joy. "Whatever is good and perfect," the Bible says, "comes down to us from God" (James 1:17). So when we act according to his ways, we experience joy because his ways reflect the ultimate good and perfect God. Being honest brings us joy because he is true. Staying sexually pure brings us joy because he is holy. Treating others justly brings us joy because he is just. His commands for us to act in certain ways flow out of who he is and how he himself acts. His ways simply reflect who he is—perfectly right—and that way of living brings joy: It provides for us and protects us.

God is by no means a legalist. He gave us his laws and instructions as boundaries to tell us what is right and wrong and that living out his ways are for our good. He wants us to relate to him and live like him because that will bring joy to our lives. And that brings him joy. "I have told you this," Jesus said, "so that my joy may be in you and that your joy may be complete" (John 15:11 NIV).

27.

IS GOD VIOLENT?

Anyone reading the Old Testament will acknowledge that it describes a people who endure great tragedy and triumph, which includes many acts of violence. There are stories of treachery, terrorism, rape, murder, war, slaughter of the innocent, torture, enslavement, and mass killings. While the Bible documents this violent behavior, we can't assume God always approves. But the question is, is he violent? Does he engage in violent acts?

WHY DOES GOD COMMIT VIOLENCE?

The short answer is yes. But unless we have a context for God's violence, we risk misunderstanding his nature.* He is merciful and loving (Psalm 103:8). He is holy and righteous (Psalm 145:17 and Revelation 3:7). He is also fair and just. "O LORD, you are righteous, and your decisions are fair. Your decrees are perfect; they are entirely worthy of our trust" (Psalm 119:137-138). "He is the Rock," Scripture states, "his deeds are perfect. Everything he does is just and fair. He is a faithful God who does no wrong; how just and upright he is!" (Deuteronomy 32:4).

So how much violence does a just God actually commit, and why? In the book of 2 Kings it is reported that during the night "the angel of the LORD went out to the Assyrian camp and killed 185,000 Assyrian soldiers" (19:35). Here we have God actually involved in the slaughter of 185,000 men, presumably while they are sleeping! Why would he commit such an atrocity? What is behind this act of violence?

First, let's recognize that we live in a world of violence that is caused not by God, but by violent humans. Every newspaper and online news source around the globe today is full of headlines and stories of greed, distrust, robberies, conflicts, killings, war, destruction, and death. And Jesus explains it is not outside circumstances that cause such evil violence in the world; rather, "from the heart come evil thoughts, murder, adultery, all

---

* See "What Is God Really Like?" on page 39.

sexual immorality, theft, lying, and slander" (Matthew 15:19). Violence in this world isn't a sociological, economic, or even pathological problem; it is a spiritual or heart problem. Sin and humans' propensity to be self-centered is at the heart of selfish violent acts.

Yet God, who is the antithesis of sin and self-centeredness, at times engages in violence because he is the ultimate protector of the innocent and judge of the unrighteous. When God killed 185,000 Assyrians he was killing soldiers who were attempting to capture Jerusalem and destroy Judah, his people. The Assyrian army under King Sennacherib had already destroyed Israel and was ready to annihilate the people of God.

Assyria was an aggressive nation that brutally tortured and killed innocent men, women, and children. The supreme commander of the evil Assyrian King Sennacherib mocked God in his reply to Judah. "What god of any nation has ever been able to save its people from my power? So what makes you think that the LORD can rescue Jerusalem from me?...Don't let your God, in whom you trust, deceive you with promises that Jerusalem will not be captured by the king of Assyria" (2 Kings 18:35; 19:10).

A heathen empire that murdered the innocent and mocked the true God deserved punishment. The Righteous Judge of the universe came to the defense of his people. Yes, God uses violence to defend, protect, and bring deserved judgment on evildoers. He said of the king of Assyria, "For my own honor and for the sake of my servant David, I will defend this city and protect it" (2 Kings 19:34).

THE DEFENDER AND THE JUDGE

We should not think less of God for defending the righteous and judging the unrighteous. He is our hero for coming to the aid of the oppressed. What was he to do when, before creation, his holiness, justice, and power were challenged by Satan? Should he have stood by and not fought against rebellion and evil? No, it was right and just that he resort to violence to cast Satan from heaven. And it is right and just that he continue that war until he conquers Satan, all evil, and death so that one day there will be eternal peace (see Revelation 12–21).

God is merciful and loving, "slow to get angry and filled with unfailing love" (Psalm 103:8), yet he will not stand by and let evil go unjudged. "He is coming to judge the earth," the Bible says. "He will judge the world with justice, and the nations with his truth" (Psalm 96:13). God is just, and he uses violence to execute perfect justice—which in the end will bring perfect and eternal peace. And Christ is our hero and coming King—the one who is the "Prince of Peace. His government and its peace will never end. He will rule with fairness and justice from the throne of his ancestor David for all eternity. The passionate commitment of the LORD of Heaven's Armies will make this happen!" (Isaiah 9:6-7).

28.

IS RELIGION THE REAL CAUSE OF VIOLENCE IN THE WORLD?

I s religion behind all the violence in the world? Is the cause of all fighting somehow rooted in religious beliefs? Some say it is.

For example, God accepted Abel's offering and rejected that of Cain. "This," the Bible says, "made Cain very angry" (Genesis 4:5). Later Cain killed Abel. The first act of violence among humans that the Bible records was rooted in a religious issue. Many more acts of violence have followed throughout human history that are directly or indirectly related to religion.

Author and professor J. Harold Ellens's 2007 book *The Destructive Power of Religion* points to religion as the cause of violence in the world. The following web post introduces the book:

> Whether they fly airplanes into the World Trade Center or Pentagon, blow up ships, ports, and federal buildings, kill doctors and nurses at abortion clinics, exterminate contemporary Palestinians, or kill Israeli soldiers with suicide bombs, destructive religionists are all shaped by the same unconscious apocalyptic metaphors, and by the divine example and imperative to violence.[14]

From Cain to the Egyptian enslavement of the children of Israel to the religious Crusades of the eleventh, twelfth, and thirteenth centuries to present-day conflicts around the world, religion is seen as more a force for violence than of peace. Perhaps that is why an atheist like the late author and speaker Christopher Hitchens wrote, "Religion poisons everything."[15] Nineteenth-century atheist Friedrich Nietzsche had an equally degrading view of Christianity when he said, "It seeks to work the ultimate corruption, nothing untouched by its depravity, it had turned every value into worthlessness, and every truth into a lie, and every integrity into baseness of the soul."[16]

But is religion, and specifically Christianity, the cause of violence in the world? There is no doubt that violent wars have been fought in the name of God. But religion is not the only, or even the greatest, cause of violence in the world. We must also recognize that the greatest bloodshed in the twentieth century was perpetrated by secular regimes such as Marxist governments. At least 100 million people were killed in communist China, the Soviet Union, Cambodia, and other communist regimes in the twentieth century alone.

LOOKING AT ULTIMATE CAUSES

But it is not Christianity, religion, or secular ideology that is the *ultimate* cause of violence—rather it stems from the self-centered hearts of humans.* Jesus said it is not outside circumstances or conflicting religious views that cause evil and violence in the world—rather, "from the heart come evil thoughts, murder, adultery, all sexual immorality, theft, lying, and slander. These are what defile you" (Matthew 15:19-20).

The self-centered heart of humans, which fosters greed, envy, jealousy, pride, and hatred, is what has caused destructive violence in the world. And unfortunately this is often done in the name of religion. In fact, it was envy and a prideful heart that caused Satan to rise up in violence against God. So violence has been with us from the very beginning. Yet that is not what the religion of Jesus was about.

Left unchecked, human nature will always revert to self-serving ways that seek to gain at another's expense. And people will often use violence to achieve their goals. But on the opposite side of the equation is Jesus' message of making the interest and care of others as important as your own. This is, in fact, at the center of his teaching, and it represents the very heart of God. Jesus said, "Do for others what you would like them to do for you. This is a summary of all that is taught in the law and the prophets" (Matthew 7:12 NLT).

Although there are those past and present who, under the banner of religion, have waged war, enslaved people, and violently tried to dominate others, this is not the way of true Christianity. Why should Christianity be blamed when people act *contrary* to the teachings and example of Jesus? For it is Christ who is the "Prince of Peace" (Isaiah 9:6), and throughout

---

* See "What Causes People to Sin Today?" on page 54.

history there is no doubt that devoted Christ-followers have been a powerful redemptive force for peace and good in our world.

It is Jesus' worldview that has led his followers to promote peace and humanitarian efforts to establish protection of infants and the unborn, child labor laws, separation of church and state, liberty and justice, and care for those in need all across the world. It is Jesus and his brand of religion that has turned away from violence and has fostered more good and provided more positive contributions to society than any other force in history.

29.

IS GOD GENOCIDAL?

To commit genocide is to deliberately kill a large racial, political, or cultural group of people, especially those of a particular ethnic group or nation. The word *genocide* is a combined Greek and Latin word meaning "race killing."

The atrocities of Hitler and the Nazi army upon the Jewish people were genocide. The Nazis rounded up and murdered some 6 million Jews between 1938 and 1945. There were over 2 million genocidal killings of Cambodians by Pol Pot's Khmer Rouge army between 1975 and 1979. Over a period of 100 days in 1994 perhaps 800,000 Tutsis in Rwanda were brutally murdered by militia of the Hutu tribe. And between 1992 and 1995 the Serbs of Bosnia-Herzegovina committed "ethnic cleansing" by murdering over 200,000 Muslims in Bosnia. These are just a few examples of genocide humans have perpetrated on one another in recent history.

Such merciless killings of groups of people are repulsive. They go against our sense of morality, freedom, and justice. So could God engage in such atrocities against a people or race? Is it possible that he is genocidal?

In the book of Deuteronomy the children of Israel were told to "completely destroy the Hittites, Amorites, Canaanites, Perizzites, Hivites, and Jebusites, just as the LORD your God has commanded you" (Deuteronomy 20:17). Years later "Joshua conquered the whole region...He completely destroyed everyone in the land, leaving no survivors, just as the LORD, the God of Israel, had commanded" (Joshua 10:40). Because of this, people such as atheist Christopher Hitchens have accused God of genocide and said that the Canaanites were "pitilessly driven out of their homes to make room for the ungrateful and mutinous children of Israel."[17] So is he a merciless deity that in anger wipes out entire races of people?

GOD'S MOTIVATION

First, any killing by God in the Old Testament was not genocide. He was motivated by moral concerns, not race. Genocide simply is not within his nature. In answering the questions "What Is God Really Like?" and "Is God Violent?"* we discovered that he is merciful and loving (Psalm 103:8), holy and righteous (Psalm 145:17 and Revelation 3:7), and fair and just (Psalm 119:137-138). God does not rush to judgment—he is "slow to get angry and filled with unfailing love" (Psalm 103:8). But he will "judge the world with justice, and the nations with his truth" (Psalm 96:13). It is not in his nature to be unjust.

God could not be a perfect and loving God without equally being a just God who judges perfectly. He cannot look the other way when wickedness is committed and still be good. Theologian J.I. Packer helps us see this point clearly:

> Would a God who did not care about the difference between right and wrong be a good and admirable being? Would a God who puts no distinctions between the beasts of history, the Hitlers and Stalins (if we dare use names), and his own saints, be morally praiseworthy and perfect? Moral indifference would be imperfection in God, not a perfection. But not to judge the world would be to show moral indifference. The final proof that God is a perfect moral being, not indifferent to questions of right and wrong, is the fact that he has committed himself to judge the world.[18]

God judges rightly because he is perfect, holy, and loving. For him to act differently would make him less than God.

GOD'S REASONS

Secondly, we must determine why God commanded that an entire people be destroyed. Moses told the children of Israel that "God will drive these nations out ahead of you only because of their wickedness, and to fulfill the oath he swore to your ancestors Abraham, Isaac, and Jacob" (Deuteronomy 9:5). Ridding the land of the Canaanites that was promised to Abraham wasn't because of anything the children of Israel did or because they were living true to God—they were not. The land was to go to them because God promised it to Abraham.

---

* See pages 39 and 75.

Additionally, the Canaanites were destroyed because of their wickedness. They were idolaters. They engaged in incest, temple prostitution, adultery, homosexuality, and bestiality. They also molested and sacrificed children. They were a depraved people. Yet God was patient and extended mercy to them even in their despicable sin. The people of Canaan were given over 400 years to repent of their wicked ways (Genesis 15:16). God had nothing against the them as a people—he did, however, take issue with their depraved and evil behavior.

Even so, he was willing to save those within Canaan that were righteous. In fact he saved Rahab in Jericho because she was a righteous individual. God does eventually bring judgment upon all that are unrepentant of their sin. And the people of Canaan were no different. This does not make him genocidal; it simply reflects his holy justice and righteous judgment.*

One of the most common objections against God is the prevalence of evil in the world. Why doesn't he stop evil and suffering? And yet when he does act to stop evil, such as with the judgment of the Canaanites, people complain he is too harsh. But if a holy, righteous, all-knowing God really exists, wouldn't we expect him to measure out judgment to evildoers? Even if we can't fully understand *why* he had the Canaanites destroyed, we can be confident he has good reasons. God is God, and we are not. "'My thoughts are nothing like your thoughts,' says the LORD. 'And my ways are far beyond anything you could imagine'" (Isaiah 55:8).

While we may struggle at times understanding God's methods of justice and judgment, by faith we must acknowledge him as the awesome and holy God that he is. As King David said,

> O God, your ways are holy. Is there any god as mighty as you? You are the God of great wonders! You demonstrate your awesome power among the nations. By your strong arm, you redeemed your people (Psalm 77:13-15).

---

* For a more exhaustive treatment see chapter 13, "Is God a Genocidal Bully?" in *Is God Just a Human Invention?*. For more information about *Is God Just a Human Invention?*, see the back of this book.

30.

HOW CAN A LOVING GOD
SEND PEOPLE TO HELL?

Many people think it just doesn't seem right that God would condemn some people to a fiery place of damnation. God is love, and eternally punishing people doesn't quite fit with that, right? So how can a loving God send people to hell?

To begin, it would be helpful to understand where God is thought to be sending people. The majority of Americans believe in a place called hell. Many consider it a place of eternal punishment of "fire and brimstone"—like a fiery torture chamber. But is this what hell is—an eternal furnace of sorts where people are tortured forever? Just what is it?

CLARIFYING THE WORDS OF SCRIPTURE

To understand the teaching of Scripture we must understand when words are used literally or figuratively. If we don't, we can easily misunderstand the teaching. Jesus referred to hell as a place where there is fire, which normally produces light (Mark 9:48). At the same time he referred to it as a place of "outer darkness" (Matthew 22:13). It seems reasonable that these words are figurative. If a literal meaning were attached to them, darkness and light from fire would cancel each other out. Jesus often used metaphors in his teachings, and here we believe he was giving a word picture of the indescribable nature of hell.

Hell is better understood by what is *not* there. Paul describes it as a place "away from the presence of the Lord and from the glory of His power" (2 Thessalonians 1:9 NASB). Try to imagine a place away from the God of relationships. A place without him is a place without relationships, without love, without joy, peace, beauty, satisfaction, contentment, acceptance, affection, fulfillment, laughter, and everything else that is called good. That would be hell—literally. A place void of all that God is would be a place of eternal aloneness—a place called hell. We believe that the "outer darkness" Jesus referred to describes this complete absence of relationship. And this eternal aloneness would be the source of inde-scribable anguish.

Likewise, we believe that the metaphor of eternal fire to describe hell suggests the decomposition of the soul. It describes a never-ending disin-tegration of all that is good in a person. Truth is, we are living souls that are becoming something. We are either becoming a person who is unself-ishly loving God and others, which is real life, or we are selfishly loving ourselves, which is real death. Pastor, apologist, and author Tim Keller provides insight into this concept:

> Even in this life we can see the kind of soul disintegration that self-centeredness creates. We know how selfishness and self-absorption leads to perceiving bitterness, nauseating envy, paralyzing anxiety, paranoid thoughts, and the mental deni-als and distortions that accompany them. Now ask the ques-tion: "What if when we die we don't end, but spiritually our life extends on into eternity?" Hell, then, is the trajectory of a soul, living a self-absorbed, self-centered life, going on and on forever.[19]

Jesus warned us that self-centered living would end in loss. "If you try to keep your life for yourself, you will lose it. But if you give up your life for me, you will find true life. And how do you benefit if you gain the whole world but lose or forfeit your own soul in the process?" (Luke 9:24-25 NLT). A self-centered life is like existing as a living dead person.

GOD'S TRUE DESIRE

Hell then is a place absent of relationship, which is absolute alone-ness. Hell is a place of perpetual disintegration of the soul into greater and greater self-centeredness. It is hard to imagine the anguish of such a place—the absolute aloneness of the living dead. Yet is a loving God send-ing people to that place?

Scripture makes it clear that God "does not want anyone to be destroyed, but wants everyone to repent" (2 Peter 3:9). He loves the whole world and died that we might experience his presence and all the joy and goodness that brings. But he will not force us to love him and enjoy a relationship with him. So actually, God doesn't send people to hell; they make a free choice to reject him. He forces no one into a relationship with him. And his giving humans free choice has opened up consequences that can be extremely negative.* And when people choose to serve themselves instead of serving God, they ultimately choose a place void of relationship and full of self—a place called hell.

C.S. Lewis said, "All that are in hell choose it...The door to hell is locked on the inside."[20] People make the choice to serve themselves because it is uncomfortable for them to serve God and others. Heaven—where God resides—is a place of perpetual worship and service to him (see Revelation 4). A person who has chosen a self-centered life would not tolerate heaven.

———————

Hell is not where God wants anyone to end up. He won't force them to choose him in order to have an eternity of joy with him. He simply offers himself as their salvation from an eternity without him. "I am the resurrection and the life," Jesus says. "Those who believe in me, even though they die like everyone else, will live again. They are given eternal life for believing in me and will never perish" (John 11:25-26 NLT).†

———————

* See "Where Did Evil Come From?" on page 51.

† For a more comprehensive biblical view of hell see chapter 12, "Is Hell a Divine Torture Chamber?" in *Is God Just a Human Invention?*, mentioned in the back pages of this book.

31.

DOES GOD PUNISH PEOPLE THROUGH NATURAL DISASTERS?

The small nation of Haiti was devastated in 2010 by a massive earthquake. In 2005, Hurricane Katrina ravaged the Gulf Coast of the United States. The 2011 earthquake and tsunami in Japan caused enormous destruction. Each year thousands of earthquakes, tsunamis, hurricanes, floods, typhoons, cyclones, tornadoes, volcanoes, droughts, and mudslides cause billions of dollars in property damage and kill tens of thousands of men, women, children, and animals. The Bible says that Christ "holds all creation together" (Colossians 1:17)...so is he responsible for these natural disasters? Is God punishing people by sending them earthquakes, volcanoes, hurricanes, floods, and every kind of natural catastrophe?

The Old Testament records incidents where God withheld rain from Israel (1 Kings 17:1), sent plagues upon Egypt (Exodus 1:19-20), and opened up the ground to swallow the household of Korah, who was rebelling against Moses (Numbers 16:29-33). We see that Jesus had control of the weather, when he calmed the storm for his disciples (Luke 8:24). God is fully in control of every atom of the universe. Because of this, there are those today who say he uses the natural elements to accomplish his will, especially in executing judgment upon nations, cities, and towns and villages.

God is indeed sovereign over all the universe. He is in ultimate control of all his creation. Yet that doesn't mean he chooses to manipulate all natural phenomena. He unquestionably has the power to intervene in the natural world—and he has done so and does so now—but he doesn't necessarily cause every climate change, for instance. Nor is every natural disaster an "act of God."

In Genesis we learn that the world was a perfect place. But after humans rebelled against God (sinned), the natural consequence was death—separation from God, who is the very sustainer of life and all that is good. In this separation Adam and Eve encountered a world where life was hard and natural disasters happened. The planet seemed to undergo a transition to violence. And ever since, cold air and warm air collide, turbulent weather patterns form, tornadoes twist, hurricanes swirl, rains fall, floods come, the earth shifts, the ground shakes, volcanoes erupt. Today the earth experiences 2000 thunderstorms at any one time. Further, our planet receives a shocking 100 lightning strikes per second—3.6 trillion strikes per year![21] We live on a violent earth.

But God is no more pleased with natural disasters than we are. And he will one day bring peace to a violent earth. Scripture says that "all creation is waiting eagerly for that future day when God will reveal who his children really are" and "when it will join God's children in glorious freedom from death and decay. For we know that all creation has been groaning as in the pains of childbirth up to the present time" (Romans 8:19-21).

Meteorologists tell us that floods are the number-one killer among natural disasters. Perhaps the message isn't that God is punishing those who are swept away, but rather that we need to be more careful where we build our businesses and homes. Modern construction has enabled levees and other control devices to be built that have opened up millions of acres for communities to grow around the world. And when these devices overflow or break, low-lying communities are devastated. This isn't to suggest that God can't speak through natural disasters nor judge people by them. But this planet follows the laws of physics and nature. So it is wise when natural tragedy strikes not to cast blame on either the victims or on God.

Life on this earth is uncertain—nothing is guaranteed. Good things happen to bad people and bad things happen to good people. Jesus said that God "gives his sunlight to both the evil and the good, and he sends rain on the just and the unjust alike" (Matthew 5:45). When natural disasters strike, rather than wondering if God is punishing us personally, it is better to follow Peter's advice to "humble yourselves under the mighty power of God, and in his good time he will honor you. Give all your worries and cares to God, for he cares about you" (1 Peter 5:7).

32.

WHY DOES GOD ALLOW SUFFERING?

Books could not hold the chronicles of all the suffering humans have experienced since the dawn of time. As Bart Ehrman, agnostic professor and author of *God's Problem,* asks,

> We live in a world in which a child dies every five seconds of starvation. Every minute there are twenty-five people who die because they do not have clean water to drink. Every hour 700 people die of malaria. Where is God in all this?[22]

How can you explain all the misery and suffering in the world if God is truly sovereign and in control of things? Is there an answer to why God allows suffering?

Some say that suffering is "God's punishment for sin" or "a test of faith" or "the devil's attack on humans and Planet Earth" or "God's means of redemption" or "a huge mystery, and we have no right to question God why it happens." Yet we believe the question is a valid one that deserves a response. We acknowledge that a brief discussion on this subject is inadequate, but we hope to provide at least some perspective.

First, we don't think there is any logical explanation that somehow satisfies the profound emotional cry for a solution to the horrific problem of pain and suffering. So we admit that reason and philosophical discourse cannot fully answer the cries of the heart. But this does not mean we should not think deeply about it. All things considered, we believe the Christian worldview provides the most intellectually satisfying and emotionally fulfilling response to the problem of suffering and evil.

From the very beginning, God has given humans created in his image the power of free choice or free will.* From a human perspective there was a great risk in God's doing this—humans might choose their own way and not his. And of course they did. That might not sound that earth-shattering on the surface, but it is.

---

* See "Where Did Evil Come From?" on page 51.

If you accept the premise that "whatever is good and perfect comes down to us from God" (James 1:16), then you probably accept the notion that experiencing a life of joy, peace, gentleness, beauty, kindness, love, and all that is called good is dependent upon and the result of being in relationship with God and living in accordance with his ways. So then, if a finite human created to be in relationship with God chooses against that relationship, what is the alternative? A life without joy, peace, love, goodness, and so on is a life opposite of God's—resulting in a life of pain and suffering.

Imagine that the very first family of fish was intelligent beings with eternal souls. Of course as fish they were designed to live in water with gills that breathed "good oxygen" from Lake Paradise. But what if this first fish couple chose to "live" outside their perfect home of Lake Paradise? As we know, this would be a tragic mistake. Fish are not designed to breathe the open air because that is "bad oxygen" for them. And if they do they will experience pain and suffering. But because these particular fish have eternal souls they experience the suffering of a "living death." And what about all the offspring of these fish? The "living death" experience is passed to every new fish born outside of Lake Paradise. Is this tragedy the fault of the fish Creator? Or is the suffering caused by the first fish that chose to live contrary to their design and outside of the Paradise in relationship with their Maker?

Granted, this illustration doesn't answer all the difficult details of why suffering happens. But perhaps it helps us to remember that an infinite Creator, who is perfect, holy, and good, created humans to enjoy life in relationship with him. God gave the first couple a very good thing—the power to choose between unselfishly loving him and believing that he knew what was best (a very good thing)…or selfishly loving themselves and believing *they* knew what was best (a very bad thing). What God wanted was for finite humans to trust that he (the infinite God) knew what was best for them (finite humans). He wanted them to unselfishly put him first and learn that his way of living was the way of joy, peace, and goodness. If the first couple had followed that way they would have avoided pain and suffering.

WHAT GOD IS DOING ABOUT SUFFERING

To a degree, we may craft a theological or philosophical answer for why there is suffering and why free choice has in effect allowed it. Yet in many respects the intensity of human suffering is simply too emotionally overwhelming for reason or logic to provide a thoroughly satisfying answer. And actually, the Bible by and large doesn't directly address the question of why there is suffering. However, from the first book of Genesis to the last book of Revelation it does tell us what God is doing about it. *He has not ignored suffering; he is redeeming the world from it.*

When humans chose to reject God and his ways it did bring immeasurable pain and suffering to humanity. But it wasn't only humanity that suffered. God did not have an impersonal response to suffering. He suffered as well, for the Bible says, "It broke his heart" (Genesis 6:6). While it is true that he is "slow to get angry and filled with unfailing love" (Psalm 103:8), he does get angry. He is angry that sin brings pain and suffering to his creation. He is angry that death has separated him from the children he created. He is angry with his archenemy, who holds the power of death.

But in his holy anger and unfailing love he has taken action. Long ago he promised Abraham that through his descendants he would provide a final solution to suffering, pain, and death. "In that day," he promised the children of Abraham, "he will remove the cloud of gloom, the shadow of death that hangs over the earth. He will swallow up death forever! The Sovereign LORD will wipe away all tears. He will remove forever all insults and mockery against his land and people" (Isaiah 25:7-8).

God's solution to all suffering meant that he would take the form of a human and also suffer. Jesus would experience the full weight of human suffering—that is, hunger, betrayal, rejection, loneliness, and the torturous death of crucifixion. So in a real sense God knows what it is to suffer, and he sympathizes with us (see Hebrews 2:18; 4:15). But he did not leave it there. Jesus would rise again to reclaim fallen humans from the power of death and from the power of his ancient enemy, the devil himself. "For only as a human being could he [Jesus] die, and only by dying could he break the power of the devil, who had the power of death" (Hebrews 2:14).

God is not about to allow Satan to destroy his creation. He has a redemption and restoration plan. "Christ was raised first," the Bible says,

> then when Christ comes back, all his people will be raised.
> After that the end will come, when he will turn the Kingdom
> over to God the Father, having put down all enemies of every
> kind. For Christ must reign until he humbles all his enemies

> beneath his feet. And the last enemy to be destroyed is death (1 Corinthians 15:23-26 NLT).

> The Son of God appeared for this purpose, to destroy the works of the devil (1 John 3:8 NASB).

> When he has conquered all things, the Son will present himself to God, so that God, who gave his Son authority over all things, will be utterly supreme over everything everywhere (1 Corinthians 15:28 NLT).

God of course knew that we humans would not trust that he knew what was best for us and we would choose our own way. But if love was to be genuine it had to be of our own choosing. He was willing to allow us to choose even if it brought him great pain to redeem us back to himself.

You can hear the sadness in Jesus' voice as he laments that the nation of Israel, as a representative of the human race, was rejecting him and his ways: "O Jerusalem, Jerusalem, the city that kills the prophets and stones God's messengers! How often I have wanted to gather your children together as a hen protects her chicks beneath her wings, but you wouldn't let me" (Matthew 23:37). Isn't it amazing how God respects and honors our choices even though he understands fully the devastating consequences they will have upon him and us? That in and of itself demonstrates how much our relational God highly honors the reality that love is a choice.

But with all that said, there is still left this nagging issue: If suffering is the natural consequence of free choice, then why do the innocent have to suffer? And why hasn't God done something sooner to end it all? If he is going to finally conquer death, why is it taking him so long to do it? That is the subject of our next question.

33.

WHY DOESN'T GOD STOP THE SUFFERING NOW?

This world is full of suffering and pain, and God does allow it. And while we may understand to a point why God had to allow suffering,* why doesn't he end it now? Why has he allowed it to continue so long? That is a troubling question.

A perfect and holy God created a perfect world. He "looked over all he made, and he saw that it was excellent in every way" (Genesis 1:31 NLT). Yet not for long. Because of free will, humans had a choice of God's way or their way. They chose their way, and sin and evil entered the world. The perfect paradise God had created was destroyed. And from that moment forward—multiplied thousands of years—hunger, disease, hatred, wars, and untold heartache have plagued the human race. It is true God has promised to redeem those who trust in his Son for salvation and to restore creation back to his original design. But why is God taking so long to correct the tragic mess humans have made of this world?

A DIFFICULT QUESTION

We confess that we cannot satisfactorily explain why God has allowed suffering for as long as he has. We agree with agnostic Bart Ehrman that the question "Where is God in all this?" which we mentioned in the previous chapter, is a valid one, even though we disagree with his answers and conclusions.

But why God is taking *so long* to end pain and suffering is truly a perplexing question. Over 2500 years ago Habakkuk, a prophet of Judah, had the same question. He lived at a time when Judah was violent and wicked, and many innocents suffered. The prophet asked, "How long, O LORD, must I call for help? But you do not listen! 'Violence is everywhere!' I cry, but you do not come to save. Must I forever see these evil deeds? Why must I watch all this misery?" (Habakkuk 1:1-3). It appeared to Habakkuk that God was ignoring the problem of pain and suffering.

---

* See "Why Does God Allow Suffering?" on page 89.

Job had a similar complaint. He had a large stock of animals that were stolen, and all his farmhands were killed. His house was destroyed and all of his children died. He contracted a terrible case of boils from head to foot. And as he sat in misery scraping his running sores with broken pieces of pottery, the only comfort and advice he got from his wife was, "Curse God and die" (Job 2:9).

Instead, Job cursed the day he was born and asked, "Why is life given to those with no future, those destined by God to live in distress?...I have no peace, no quietness. I have no rest; instead, only trouble comes" (Job 3:23,26 NLT). He could not understand why God would allow such suffering for those without a future.

King David had his questions for God too. He was misunderstood, mistreated, and betrayed, and he suffered at the hands of his enemies. He cried out,

> O Lord, how long will you forget me? Forever? How long will you look the other way? How long must I struggle with anguish in my soul, with sorrow in my heart every day?...Turn and answer me, O Lord my God! (Psalm 13:1-3).

What is God's answer? Why doesn't he stop the madness? Today in the twenty-first century violence is everywhere. Life is also given to those with no real future. We see the misery and hopelessness of the starving and broken. Where is God? Why does he let it go on?

EVEN JESUS ASKED WHY

One final question before we offer an answer. Jesus, who was very God and very man, also had a question. He knew he was to suffer and die a cruel death for the sins of the world. Yet just before his crucifixion he prayed, "My Father! If it is possible, let this cup of suffering be taken away from me. Yet I want your will to be done, not mine" (Matthew 26:39). It is not strange that on a human level Jesus didn't want to suffer. It is clear that he was struggling with the knowledge that he would experience great pain and suffering. Humanly he didn't want to endure the torturous death of the cross—yet he would do it for his Father.

And hours later Jesus asks perhaps the most perplexing question of all time. While he is hanging on the cross, dying a hideous death, he musters the strength to ask, "My God, my God, why have you abandoned me?"

(Matthew 27:46). What a question to come from the Son of God to his Father! Jesus was actually quoting Psalm 22:1, where King David asked that question. David followed up that question with, "Why are you so far away when I groan for help? Every day I call to you, my God, but you do not answer. Every night you hear my voice, but I find no relief" (Psalm 22:1-2).

It is as if Jesus spoke on behalf of the entire human race with this question: "Why, God, have you abandoned us?" It was as if his cry was amplified to echo back to the expulsion of the first couple from the Garden of Eden and forward to the end of time, asking, *"Why don't you do something about this now?"*

GOD DESIRES MORE RELATIONSHIPS

We don't know if or how God answered his Son on the cross. The questions of Habakkuk, Job, and David were left unexplained. Search all of Scripture and you will find very few answers. The apostle Peter suggests that God is waiting for more people to come to him. "The Lord isn't really being slow about his promise to return," Peter says. "No, he is being patient for your sake. He does not want anyone to perish, so he is giving more time for everyone to repent...the Lord is waiting so that people have time to be saved" (2 Peter 3:9,15).

It's true that the longer God waits to return, the more people are coming to him. Studies by Operation World reported by the book *Perspectives* shows that by 1887, after 100 years of Christian missionary work around the world, there were 3 million Protestant converts out of a world population of a billion and a half. Today, over 100 years later, those numbers have dramatically changed.

Christianity may have declined as a proportion of the West's population, but this is not so in other major population areas of the world. For example, in 1900 there were 8 million Christians in Africa; by 2000 there were 351 million. Christianity has now become the major religion across sub-Saharan Africa. In 1900 there were 22 million Christians in Asia; by 2005 there were around 370 million. From 1900 to 2000 evangelicals grew in Latin America from about 700,000 to over 55 million. And more Muslims are turning to Christ in the Middle East than at any other time in history. The 2006 Operation World report summarized it thus:

> Evangelical Christianity is currently the fastest growing religious movement in the world today. Evangelical growth

represents more than double the growth rate of the next closest religion (Islam) and more than triple the world's population growth rate.[23]

Does this mean that as long as the earth is being populated and people are coming to Christ, God will wait to bring an end to it all? We don't
know. But God does, and it seems clear he has simply chosen not to fully
explain why he has allowed evil, suffering, pain, and death to last as long
as it has.

Listen to what God said to Habakkuk. "Look around at the nations;
look and be amazed! For I am doing something in your own day, something you wouldn't believe even if someone told you about it" (Habakkuk 1:5). Yes, he had a plan then and he still does. He had a reason for
doing what he was doing, he just wasn't going to explain it all to Habakkuk. Sure—God could explain to us today why there is suffering and why
he is taking centuries to accomplish his ultimate goal of "reconciling the
world to himself" (2 Corinthians 5:19). He could explain why he hasn't yet
recreated this world as a place where "there will be no more death or sorrow or crying or pain" (Revelation 21:4). But he has chosen not to explain
it to us. Yet that doesn't mean we don't have an answer.

FOCUSING ON GOD HIMSELF

It seems that God gave Habakkuk understanding of how he wanted
him—and all of us—to respond. Rather than trying to figure out the
details of his *plan*, God wants us to focus on him as a *person*. He told
Habakkuk that

> these things I plan won't happen right away. Slowly, steadily,
> surely, the time approaches when the vision will be fulfilled.
> If it seems slow, wait patiently, for it will surely take place. It
> will not be delayed. Look at the proud! They trust in them-
> selves, and their lives are crooked; but the righteous will live
> by their faith (Habakkuk 2:3-4 NLT).

There it is: God wants us to trust in him personally even if we don't
understand his plan. Job finally got the same message—that he was to put
faith in the person of God. Job said to him, "I know that you can do anything, and no one can stop you. You asked 'Who is this that questions my
wisdom with such ignorance?' It is I—and I was talking about things I

knew nothing about, things far too wonderful for me" (Job 42:2-3). And how did he come to the conclusion that God's ways and his plans were beyond his comprehension? By knowing God the person. "I had only heard about you before," Job said, "but now I have seen you with my own eyes" (Job 42:5). His focus was no longer on a plan, but in a person whom he trusted to know what he was doing.

King David understood the message that he was to live by faith in the person of God too. Right after he asked God, "Why have you abandoned me?" he declared, "Yet you are holy, enthroned on the praises of Israel. Our ancestors trusted in you, and you rescued them...they trusted in you and were never disgraced" (Psalm 22:3-5). Read the entirety of Psalm 22 and you will find David got the message. He may not have understood why God delayed in making all things right, but he believed he was good and knew what he was doing.

And while Jesus as God knew that his suffering was the only solution for sin, suffering, and death, he modeled for us what we must do—place our faith and trust in God, who does all things right in his right timing. Peter said,

> God called you to do good, even if it means suffering, just as Christ suffered for you. He is your example, and you must follow in his steps. He never sinned, nor even deceived anyone. He did not retaliate when he was insulted, nor threaten revenge when he suffered. He left his case in the hands of God [he kept entrusting himself to God] who always judges fairly (1 Peter 2:21-23).

We may not understand God's plan, but we can trust in his person. He is faithful and just and always judges rightly. And he is always with us. Jesus said, "I am leaving you with a gift—peace of mind and heart. And the peace I give is a gift the world cannot give. So don't be troubled or afraid" (John 14:27). He prayed to his Father to send us his Spirit—the Holy Spirit to guide us, comfort us, and be with us no matter what happens. Jesus said, "Be sure of this: I am with you always, even to the end of the age" (Matthew 28:20).

34.

Does God Have Feelings and Emotions?

Emotions are a state of feeling or the experiencing of certain feelings based on internal or external influences. There are many theories, going back to Plato and Aristotle, as to what emotions are and where they come from. We, as humans, and even animals have emotions. Some of the most basic human emotions include *joy*—being glad, pleased, satisfied, happy, contented, fulfilled, complete, and so on; *sad*—grieved, dejected, heartbroken, depressed, and so on; *excited*—ecstatic, energetic, thrilled, aroused, and so on; *scared*—frightened, terrified, anxious, tense, and so on; *angry*—irritated, upset, furious, mad, displeased, and so on; *tender*—loving, warm-hearted, intimate, sympathetic, and so on.

Many theorists define some emotions as basic and others as complex. And there is seemingly no consensus on how to determine which are which. Yet it is universally agreed we are complex emotional beings who have healthy emotions, unhealthy emotions, and even emotional disorders. Where did we get our emotions? Did God create us with them because he has feelings and emotions too?

In the book of Genesis it says that "God said, 'Let us make human beings in our own image, to be like us'" (1:26). So if he has emotions perhaps he did pass them on to us. He is infinite in his eternal existence, he is all-powerful, ever-present, knows everything, and so on.* As finite humans we don't bear those characteristics of God. We know he is also holy, perfect, and righteous. He can do nothing sinful or wrong. And we know as sinful humans we didn't inherit his holy nature either. But we did inherit his relational image.

God exists as relationship—three persons who share the one substance

---

* See "What Is God Really Like" on page 39.

and essence of being God.* Scripture refers to our Creator as the "God who is passionate about his relationship with you" (Exodus 34:14 NLT). And as a relational God he expresses relational emotions. For example, even before he took on human form in the person of Jesus, the Bible tells us some of the emotions he expressed.

- satisfied (Genesis 1:31)
- brokenhearted (Genesis 6:6)
- displeased (2 Samuel 11:27)
- joyful (Nehemiah 8:10)
- regretful (Genesis 6:6)
- caring (Deuteronomy 1:31)
- delighted (Psalm 18:19)
- angry (Exodus 32:9)
- pleasure (Psalm 16:3)
- jealous (Exodus 20:5)

Yet in all of his emotions God does no wrong (Deuteronomy 32:4). His emotions do not change him, for he is unchanging (Psalm 102:26-27 and Numbers 23:19). His emotions are an expression of his holy nature and relational heart of love. There are no emotional disorders with him. We humans, unlike God, have emotions that reflect the desires of a sinful nature; Scripture states that

> the results are very clear: sexual immorality, impurity, lustful pleasures, idolatry, sorcery, hostility, quarreling, jealousy, out-bursts of anger, selfish ambitions, dissension, division, envy... But the Holy Spirit produces this kind of fruit in our lives: love, joy, peace, patience, kindness, goodness, faithfulness, gentleness, and self-control (Galatians 5:19-23).

GODLIKE EMOTIONS

When a person is brought into relationship with God through trust

---

* See "What Does It Mean that God Is a Trinity?" on page 46.

in Christ and his sacrificial death and resurrection, the Bible says, "You must display a new nature because you are a new person, created in God's likeness—righteous, holy, and true" (Ephesians 4:24). God then begins to change our emotional responses from ungodly to godly because "his divine power...has given us everything we need for living a godly life" (2 Peter 1:3).

Our model for godlike emotions is Jesus—the God-man. God took on the form of a human and demonstrated for us how to express emotions in a godlike fashion. *Jesus experienced joy* and told his disciples, "You will be filled with my joy" (John 15:11). *He expressed righteous anger* and drove the money changers out of the temple (Matthew 21:12-13). *He felt sadness* and wept with Mary (John 11:35). And imagine the *loneliness Jesus felt* when he was rejected by his own people, abandoned by the disciples, misunderstood by his own followers, and betrayed by a close friend. Isaiah prophesied that Jesus would be "despised and rejected—a man of sorrows, acquainted with deepest grief" (Isaiah 53:3). Jesus, the Son, the second person of the Trinity, had the same human emotions that God gave us, and he expressed them perfectly. The Bible says that he "understands our weakness, for he faced all of the same testings we do, yet he did not sin" (Hebrews 4:15).

Joy is perhaps the greatest and most desired emotion of all. And nothing gives God greater joy than to have a relationship with each of us who were once lost and have been brought back to God through Christ. Jesus said, "There is joy in the presence of God's angels when even one sinner repents" (Luke 15:10). And then as we enter into eternity with God, with emotions perfectly transformed, Jesus said we will hear the Father say, "Enter into the joy of your Master" (Matthew 25:23 NASB). And for all eternity we can experience the emotions of our Creator in the way he designed us to experience them.

35.

DOES GOD LOVE EVERYONE REGARDLESS OF SEXUAL ORIENTATION?

Not long ago the news media released a picture of a man and a young boy protesting in Tulsa, Oklahoma. The young boy was holding a sign that read, *God Hates Fags.* This particular church group believes that God hates gays above all other kinds of sinners and that homosexuality should be a capital crime. On their website they assert that every tragedy in the world is linked to homosexuality, specifically society's increasing tolerance and acceptance of homosexuality as a legitimate lifestyle.

The resentment garnered by this church group is not just a problem for these few picketers. David Kinnaman, in his book *UnChristian,* indicates that, sadly, more than nine out of ten outsiders view all Christians as antihomosexual as well.

So what does God think about homosexuals? Does he love them as much as he does heterosexuals, or does he really hate "fags"?

––––––––––

First, let's look at how Jesus viewed sins. A highly respected religious leader (a Jewish Pharisee) came to Jesus in an attempt to discover who he really was. The first thing Jesus told the man was that he needed to be "born again" and that God had sent him, his Son, "into the world not to judge the world, but to save the world through him [Jesus]" (John 3:17).

Jesus went on to make a point about sin and sinners. He said there would be no judgment against the sinners who believed in him. But those sinners who refused to believe he was God's means of forgiveness would be judged. He explained that he was God's light, or salvation, and that "all who do evil hate the light and refuse to go near it for fear their sins will be exposed. But those who do what is right come to the light so others can see that they are doing what God wants" (John 3:20).

It appears the type of sins committed wasn't an issue with Jesus as long as each sinner turned his or her back on their sins (repented) and placed their trust and hope in him. In effect, the only sins he considered unforgivable were the unconfessed sins. This isn't to say that some sins aren't worse than others. Jesus said to Pilate that "the one who handed me over to you has the greater sin" (John 19:11). He taught that "much is required from those to whom much is given, and much more is required from those to whom much more is given" (Luke 12:48 NLT). Punishment and rewards may not all be equal—some sins *are* worse than others—but God's forgiveness is open equally to all those who seek it.

The apostle Paul listed out numerous sins—including sexual immorality of all kinds—that needed the forgiveness of God (see Romans 1:24-27; 1 Corinthians 6:9-10; Galatians 5:19-21; and Colossians 3:5-6). But it doesn't seem that he or the other writers of the New Testament singled out homosexuality as the vilest of sins. The judgment of God is reserved, rather, for all those who fail to place their trust in Christ as their sacrifice for sin.* So how should we treat sinners, specifically homosexuals?

———

Some years ago I (Sean) attended the Olympics with a Christian group. On one occasion I was attending to a stand that was selling Christian-oriented T-shirts. A man wearing a T-shirt covered with rainbow flags approached my booth. I inquired about the flags and asked what country it represented. "Oh, they're just a queer thing," he responded. "You see, I'm gay." In a matter-of-fact manner I asked him if people made fun of him for being gay. He responded immediately, "Oh yeah, I get demeaning statements thrown at me all the time."

I looked right at him. I could see a man who had been hurt and broken by the taunts and ridicule of others. I felt compassion for him. I said, "I'm really sorry that people have treated you that way. It's not right." He thanked me over and over again. In fact, he asked if he could get a picture of us together. He said I was the nicest person he had met at the entire Olympics.

People, no matter what their sexual orientation, are loved by God and we, as his representatives, are to love them as well. The message of Jesus is the same to all sinners, including us: "I am the resurrection and the life. Anyone who believes in me will live, even after dying. Everyone who lives in me and believes in me will never ever die" (John 11:25-26).

---

* See "Why Did Jesus Need to Die?" on page 127.

36.

DOES GOD GET INVOLVED IN POLITICS?

A survey conducted by the Gallup organization in 2010 found that one in five Americans believed that "God is actively engaged in the daily working of the world and has an economic conservative view that opposes government regulations and champions the free market."[24] So is God for reduced government, lower taxes, and a free-market economy? Is God a Democrat, a Republican, an Independent, a Socialist, or what? Does God affiliate himself with political parties or get involved in political agendas?

THE KINGDOM QUESTION

If ever there was an issue of God getting involved in politics it was in the first century. The Jewish people had endured many years under the rule of or enslaved by other governments. For centuries they had been looking for their Messiah, the Christ who would lead their nation out from tyranny into a new kingdom of rightness and glory.

When Jesus arrived on the scene, his disciples thought the time had come when their Messiah would assemble an army, defeat the Roman oppressors, and establish a new kingdom of prosperity and freedom. Of course their earthly kingdom hopes were dashed at the death of their leader. What is clear is that Jesus' followers misunderstood God's involvement in politics.

When Jesus was brought before him, the Roman governor Pontius Pilate, also tried to get some clarity on his prisoner's political views and ambitions too. He asked him if he was the King of the Jews.

"Then Jesus answered, 'I am not an earthly king. If I were, my followers would have fought when I was arrested by the Jewish leaders. But my Kingdom is not of this world'" (John 18:36 NLT). It seems the Lord of the universe didn't consider this world his kingdom. So what did he mean when he said "my Kingdom is not of this world"?

WHERE THE CONFLICT LIES

Jesus' kind of kingdom and politics wasn't about toppling the Roman

Empire. His opposition wasn't the Romans or even Jewish leaders. His opposition was Lucifer, his archenemy. Through the first humans' choice to sin and rebel against God, Satan gained control of things before the kingdom of this world could become the kingdom of God. The disciple John confirmed that "the world around us is under the control of the evil one" (1 John 5:19). Two kingdoms with two very different worldviews now exist—the kingdom of this world, with Satan as its king, and the kingdom of heaven, with God as its king. That means we are presently experiencing a conflict between the two.

The conflict isn't really political in nature, as Pilate assumed. The struggle isn't even a cultural one. The primary enemy isn't wicked people, evil regimes, or political ideology. This war is between God and his ways and Satan and his ways. We are not to be fighting against people but "against the evil rulers and authorities of the unseen world" (Ephesians 6:12).

WHAT GOD IS INTERESTED IN

But does this mean God is not involved or interested in the affairs of this world? Not at all. Jesus said to "give to Caesar [government] what belongs to Caesar" (Matthew 22:21). We are to pray for government leaders (1 Timothy 2:1-2) and honor them (1 Peter 2:13-17). But God's goal isn't to reform the kingdoms of this world through a political agenda. His plan is to conquer Satan, bring an end to suffering and death, re-create the heavens and the earth, and establish an eternal kingdom with all those who have placed their trust in him.

Let us quickly add that this doesn't mean we as Christians are not to be involved in seeing healthy social and economic change take place within our communities, cities, country, and the nations of the world. And there are biblical principles that can be applied to governmental and economic structures. Jesus said that his followers were primarily to be "the salt of the earth...the light to the world...[so that] your good deeds shine out for all to see, so that everyone will praise your heavenly Father" (Matthew 5:13-14,16).

The expression used most often to describe Jesus' heart was that he was "moved with compassion." When he saw the blind, the lepers, the sick, and the hungry he was "moved with compassion." At its core Jesus' worldview represents a focus on caring for the interests of others spiritually, physically, economically, socially, relationally—in every way. That kind of compassion toward others is a radical message now, and it was certainly the case during the time of Christ.

God may not align himself with a political party, but his mission is to redeem his lost children gripped by sin and eventually restore all of creation to its original design. And as "salt and light," his followers are not only to love God with their all, but their neighbor as themselves. And it is evident even from the beginning of the early church how social and political change resulted from Christ-followers propagating Jesus' worldview.

Faithful Christ-followers should be the best citizens of this world while not being part of it. Jesus made this distinction when he prayed that his followers would be in the world—but not part of it—"because they do not belong to the world, just as I do not belong to the world" (John 17:14). Those who live out a biblical worldview—Jesus' worldview—make the kingdom of God primary in their lives, yet they become a powerful force for good in this present world.

37.

How Can We Know God's Will in Our Lives?

One of the most common questions today among young and old alike is about knowing God's will. For years I (Sean) thought God's will was hidden from me, and my job was to try to find it—like going on a treasure hunt. But that is not the case. God has pretty much put his will out there for everyone to see. And when we know the big areas that are his will, we can more easily understand how to make wise decisions in the details of our lives, like buying a car, purchasing a home, going to a college, finding that ideal job, marrying the right person, and so on.

Scripture reveals much of God's will to us. For example:

God's will is that people come to know him and trust him. Jesus prayed to his Father and said, "This is the way to have eternal life—to know you, the only true God, and Jesus Christ, the one you sent to earth" (John 17:3). The apostle Paul said that God "wants everyone to be saved and to understand the truth" (1 Timothy 2:4). The disciple Peter told us that God "does not want anyone to be destroyed, but wants everyone to repent" (2 Peter 3:9). So it is God's will that people trust in Christ to gain a relationship with God and receive the gift of eternal life.

God's will is that his followers tell others about salvation in Christ. Jesus told his followers to "go and make disciples of all nations" (Matthew 28:19). He went on to say that "you [my followers] will be witnesses, telling people about me everywhere" (Acts 1:8). Paul said that God "gave us this wonderful message of reconciliation. So we are Christ's ambassadors" (2 Corinthians 5:19-20). It is God's will that we become what Jesus called "the salt of the earth" and "the light of the world" so that others will know the message that he is the way to God (see Matthew 5:13-16).

God's will is that people be like Christ and live pure. Scripture says that

"God knew his people in advance, and he chose them to become like his Son" (Romans 8:29). "Let the Spirit renew your thoughts and attitudes. Put on your new nature, created to be like God—truly righteous and holy" (Ephesians 4:23-24).

It is God's will that we become conformed to the image of Christ and live pure lives. The Bible says, "God's will is for you to be holy, so stay away from sexual sin. Then each of you will control his own body and live in holiness and honor" (1 Thessalonians 4:3-4). Sexual immorality is commonplace today, but it is God's will that unmarried young people remain sexually pure until marriage and that married people remain sexually faithful to one another.

God's will is that we love him and one another. Jesus said that all of Scripture hinges on this: " 'Love the Lord your God with all your heart, all your soul, and all your mind.' This is the first and greatest commandment. A second is equally important: 'Love your neighbor as yourself'" (Matthew 22:37-39). Just before he was crucified he told his disciples, "A new command I give to you: Love one another. As I have loved you, so you must love one another. By this all men will know that you are my disciples, if you love one another" (John 13:34-35 NIV).

It is God's will that we love him with our everything—making him our priority—and live out that love by loving others. And loving others includes things like accepting one another (Romans 15:7), forgiving one another (Ephesians 4:32), being patient with one another (Ephesians 4:2), living in harmony with one another (Romans 12:16), serving one another (Galatians 5:13), submitting to one another (Ephesians 5:21), comforting one another (2 Corinthians 1:4), and so on.

These are a few major areas in which Scripture reveals what God's will is. But how do we know very specifically how he is leading us to do this or that in life? First, we make sure we are doing all we can to follow the major "God's will" areas of our lives. Then we have freedom to make choices—choices that have consequences. If we make wise choices we often experience good consequences. If we make unwise choices we often suffer negative consequences. But again, deciding things like what college to attend, what person to date or marry, which car or home to purchase, what job to take, and so on isn't a right or wrong moral choice. God gives us the freedom to make those choices, and he wants us to make wise choices in those categories.

To make wise choices in the details of life it is good to rely on at least five sources:

1. *Go to God in prayer* (James 1:5). A wise person seeks his wisdom for knowing if a decision in any way violates his moral will.

2. *Go to Scripture for guidance* (2 Timothy 3:16). A wise person seeks guidance in God's Word to find strength and insight for continually seeking him and his kingdom first.

3. *Do your research* (Proverbs 18:13). Gather the facts. Developing a pro and con list to gain direction on decisions is wise.

4. *Seek godly advice from others* (Proverbs 15:22). There is great wisdom in the advice of many.

5. *Let life's experiences* teach you (Psalm 90:12). One can learn much by past experiences. A wise person does not make the same mistake twice.

God's will does not so much involve what you do, but *who you are*. If you seek to know him, put him first in your life, love others, live a Christlike life of purity, and share him with others you will be a person who is more likely to consistently make wise choices in life.

38.

DID JESUS REALLY CLAIM TO BE GOD?

Critics like atheist Richard Dawkins say it was overzealous followers of Jesus who made him out to be a deity. Dawkins writes,
"There is no good historical evidence that he even thought he was
divine."[25] These critics also point to the fact that Jesus referred to himself
as the "Son of Man" not the "Son of God." This, they say, proves he was
actually making a claim to be human, not deity. Is this true? Did Jesus
never really claim to be the Son of God?

THE MEANING OF "SON OF MAN"

It is true that Jesus referred to himself dozens of times as the "Son of
Man," but this was far from an admission of being just another human.
His use of the words "Son of Man" can be traced back to the book of Daniel. And when Daniel described the "son of man" in a vision, it is far from
a reference to a mere human. Daniel prophesied that he saw "a son of man
coming with clouds of heaven…[with] authority, honor, and sovereignty
over all the nations of the world…His rule is eternal—it will never end.
His kingdom will never be destroyed" (Daniel 7:13-14). This is not the
description of a mere mortal.

Daniel's "son of man" is a clear reference to a divine figure—the sovereign Lord whose kingdom is eternal. To claim to be the Son of Man
would actually be making a claim to divinity. And this is precisely what
Jesus was doing.

JESUS' ASSERTIONS

Jesus also made it clear that he was God, and that assertion did not
go unnoticed by the religious leaders of the day. In fact, that claim was
the very reason they tried to discredit him and, eventually, the reason
they worked to see him put to death: "So the Jewish leaders tried all the
harder to find a way to kill him. For he not only broke the Sabbath, he
called God his Father, thereby making himself equal with God" (John
5:18). Jesus went on to say, "I assure you that the time is coming, indeed

it's here now, when the dead will hear my voice—the voice of the Son of God. And those who listen will live" (John 5:25). Jesus made it abundantly clear who he was.

On more than one occasion, Jesus' clear assertion of his own deity caused his fellow Jews to try to stone him. One time he told the Jewish leaders, "Your father Abraham rejoiced at the thought of seeing my day; he saw it and was glad." His listeners became indignant and shot back, "'You are not yet fifty years old,' the Jews said to him, 'and you have seen Abraham!' 'Very truly I tell you,' Jesus answered, 'before Abraham was born, I am!' At this, they picked up stones to stone him, but Jesus hid himself, slipping away from the temple grounds" (John 8:56-59 NIV). On another occasion, when Jesus said that he was one with the Father, the Jewish leaders again picked up stones to kill him (see John 10:30-31). When Jesus asked why they wanted to kill him, they retorted, "For blasphemy! You, a mere man, claim to be God" (John 10:33).

Jesus' claim to be God is also demonstrated in his authority to forgive sins. He told a paralyzed man, "My child, your sins are forgiven," and again the religious leaders reacted with outrage. "What is he saying? This is blasphemy! Only God can forgive sins!" (Mark 2:5-7).

In the final hours before his death, Jesus made it clear—even to the Sanhedrin (the Jewish high council)—just who he was: "The high priest asked him, 'Are you the Messiah, the Son of the blessed One?' Jesus said, 'I AM…'" In response to the proclamation, "they all cried, 'He deserves to die'" (Mark 14:61-64).

All that Jesus said and did confirmed his assertion and claim to be God in the flesh.* That is why his follower John declared,

> In the beginning the Word already existed. The Word was with God, and the Word was God…the Word became human and made his home among us. He was full of unfailing love and faithfulness. And we have seen his glory, the glory of the Father's one and only Son (John 1:1,14).

---

* For a more extensive treatment of Jesus' claim to deity and the historical evidences that substantiate his claim, see *Is God Just a Human Invention?*, chapter 18. For more information about *Is God Just a Human Invention?*, see the back of this book.

39.

ISN'T IT ARROGANT TO CLAIM
THAT CHRISTIANITY IS THE
ONLY TRUE RELIGION?

A major criticism leveled at Christians is that they have the arrogance to say Christianity is the only true religion and the only way to obtain eternal life. That view seems annoyingly exclusive and intolerant to most people. Consequently, most professed Christians in America no longer claim that Christianity is exclusive. A 2008 Pew Forum survey among Americans found that 65 percent of all professed Christians say there are multiple paths to eternal life, with 80 percent of the respondents citing at least one non-Christian religion that can lead to salvation.[26]

WHO IS MAKING THE CLAIM?

So is it arrogant for a Christian today to claim he or she has the only true religion and the only teaching that leads to eternal life? This may surprise you, but we think it does come across arrogant to make the claim that one has the only true religion. It would be arrogant of anyone to make that exclusive claim unless he or she was God. But the fact of the matter is, Jesus, as the Son of God, did make the claim of being the only way to obtain eternal life. And we as Christians can avoid coming across as arrogant by making it clear it was *he* who made the "one way—one truth" claim.

Most of the religious leaders of Jesus' time also thought he came across as arrogant for saying what he said about himself. He claimed to be the Son of God who had existed eternally, who could forgive sin and give eternal life.* And Jesus would have been not just arrogant, but a deceiver, for making such an outlandish claim of exclusivity if he wasn't God—but he was. And he gave extensive evidence to substantiate his claim.

Jesus fulfilled prophecies about God's Chosen One (the Messiah), was born of a virgin, and performed many miracles before he actually said, "I

---

* See "Did Jesus Really Claim to Be God?" on page 109.

am the resurrection and the life. Those who believe in me, even though they die like everyone else, will live again. They are given eternal life for believing in me and will never perish" (John 11:25-26). He could make this seemingly arrogant declaration because he was the one and only Son of God, who could back it up. Read these words of his: "Unless you believe that I AM who I claim to be, you will die in your sins" (John 8:24). "I am the way, the truth, and the life. No one can come to the Father except through me" (John 14:6).

It was Jesus who made the exclusive claim to be the only way to God—and for good reason. No one else had the qualifications that a holy and just God would accept. Christ-followers need to be careful not to assert that *they* have a corner on truth or are the ones who have the only true religion. Rather, it is *Jesus* who is the way, the truth, and the life—his followers are simply sharing *his* message. So as Christians we need to point the matter of obtaining eternal life back to him. Our task is to spread the Good News about him. And we are wise to share that news enthusiastically, yet humbly.

Of course people can be arrogant about the truth and be right. People can be arrogant about the truth and be wrong. People can also be humble and be right; they can be humble and be wrong. The important thing for us as Christians isn't who wins the argument of who is right or wrong. That is not the point. The important thing is that we challenge people to consider Jesus for who he is and what he has to offer them. And we don't need to shy away from our belief that he is the only way. We can say as Paul did:

> I am not ashamed of this Good News about Christ. It is the power of God at work, saving everyone who believes—the Jew first and also the Gentile. This Good News tells us how God makes us right in his sight (Romans 1:16-17).

40

HOW DO WE KNOW THAT
JESUS ACTUALLY LIVED?

In recent years some people have questioned the actual existence of Jesus. Some claim that the idea of a Savior was manufactured by certain people and it ended up becoming a religion.

The problem with this thinking is that there are simply too many biblical and extrabiblical writings that attest to the real person we know as Jesus Christ, who lived and died in the first century.

AN UNTENABLE IDEA

First, it is absurd to believe that in the first century thousands of people would devote themselves to a person who never existed. By AD 100, about 65 years after Jesus had been on earth, there were some 25,000 people who called themselves Christians—named after Christ who they believed in. Many of these Christ-followers were persecuted not just by governments but by family and friends. Some even gave up their lives as martyrs for this person. Would so many people do this for a person who had never lived? And within 200 years (AD 300) the faithful band of Jesus-followers grew to over 20 million.[27] It is inconceivable that such a large following would have lasted had it been based on a phantom Christ.

THE EVIDENCE OF THE NEW TESTAMENT

Of course we also have the reliable evidence of the New Testament, which records the life and teachings of Jesus. Peter, one of his disciples, wrote a letter in the early 60s just before his martyrdom under the Emperor Nero in AD 64 or 65. He writes, "We were not making up clever stories when we told you about the powerful coming of our Lord Jesus Christ. We saw his majestic splendor with our own eyes when he received honor and glory from God the Father" (2 Peter 1:16-17). Peter was referring to the time he was present at the Mount of Transfiguration, when Jesus was visited by Moses and Elijah. He was attesting to the reality of Jesus as an eyewitness of his existence. We have 13 letters of Paul, 4 Gospels, the book of Acts, and other New Testament books that attest to the historicity of Jesus. Many of the writers of the New Testament wrote within a generation of Jesus' life and were either eyewitnesses to or familiar with eyewitness accounts of Jesus.

EVIDENCE FROM OTHER SOURCES

But beyond the New Testament accounts there are those of "secular" writers—extrabiblical writings that verify that Jesus the Christ did in fact live. For example, the historian Josephus wrote *The Antiquities of the Jews* in AD 93. In book 18, chapter 3, paragraph 3, he writes,

> About the time there lived Jesus, a wise man, if indeed one ought to call him a man...He was the Messiah. When Pilate, upon hearing him accused by men of the highest standing amongst us, had condemned him to be crucified, those who had in the first place come to love him did not give up their affection for him. [28]

Josephus also referred to "James, the brother of Jesus who was called the Christ." [29]

Pliny the Younger was one of the world's great letter-writers. Ten volumes of his correspondence have survived to the present. He wrote to the Emperor Trajan concerning the Christians of his province in AD 112, revealing how a non-Christian viewed Christianity. He writes about Christ-followers that "they were in the habit of meeting on a certain fixed day before it was light, when they sang in alternate verses a hymn to Christ, as to a god." [30]

Cornelius Tacitus, born about AD 56, became a Roman senator and is considered the most reliable of ancient historians. In his *Annals* of AD 116 he makes statements about the death of Christ as a historical fact. [31]

And many others,* like Suetonius, another Roman historian (AD 120); Lucian of Samosata, a Greek satirist (AD 170); and Mara Bar-Serapion, a Stoic philosopher (AD 70) confirmed in written history that Jesus of Nazareth lived and died. [32]

---

* For a more comprehensive and compelling case for the life and claims of Jesus see *Evidence for the Historical Jesus.* For more information about *Evidence for the Historical Jesus,* see the back of this book.

41.

HOW DID JESUS BACK UP HIS CLAIM TO BE GOD?

Jesus claimed to be the Son of God and the only way to God. And he wasn't being arrogant about it.* But did he actually give proof that he was God? How did he back up his claim to deity?

Jesus' disciples were having a little difficulty understanding just who their Master was and what he was really up to. So he made this statement: "Just believe that I am in the Father and the Father is in me. Or at least believe because of what you have seen me do" (John 14:11). Here Jesus was appealing to both his authoritative teaching on the kingdom of God and his many miracles in order to substantiate and verify he was in fact God in human form. In regard to miracles, he was in effect saying, "You are finding it hard to believe that I am God in the flesh—well, look how I as creator of all things have complete command of the forces of the universe—the weather, the human body, gravity, life, and death."

Listen to these words: "I have a greater witness than John," Jesus said, "my teachings and my miracles. The Father gave me these works to accomplish, and they prove that he sent me" (John 5:36). "The miracles I do in my Father's name speak for me" (John 10:25 NIV). Jesus' miracles became credible proof that he was who he claimed to be. So let's look at a few miracles he performed.

But first, what actually is a miracle? It can be defined as a religiously significant intervention of God in the system of natural causes. Some people contend that miracles cannot occur because it is impossible to violate the laws of nature. But those who make this contention assume that nothing exists outside of nature. They believe we live in a closed system.

However, if God exists as the Creator of the universe, then he exists outside of the laws of nature he created. He can thus step into his creation and intervene as he wills. And he has. He entered the sphere of humanity

---

* See "Did Jesus Really Claim to Be God?" on page 109.

by taking on human form in the person of Jesus. And to give us evidence he was God, Jesus performed miracles.

Here are examples of his miracle-working power from the New Testament, which documents that he was able to

- calm a storm (see Matthew 8)
- make a mute person speak (see Matthew 9)
- feed 5000 people with 5 loaves and 2 fish (see Matthew 14)
- cast out demons (see Mark 5)
- walk on water (see Mark 6)
- bring sight to the blind (see Mark 10)
- make a fig tree wither up by cursing it (see Mark 11)
- foretell the future (see Mark 14)
- heal a paralyzed man (see Luke 5)
- raise a boy from the dead (see Luke 7)
- heal incurable hemorrhaging (see Luke 8)
- cleanse lepers (see Luke 17)
- turn water into wine (see John 2)
- make the lame walk (see John 5)
- forgive sin (see John 8)
- raise a man from the dead (see John 11)

Jesus was not simply a great teacher. He was the Son of the Living God, and his miracles underscore that fact.

42

WHAT PROOF IS THERE THAT JESUS WAS THE MESSIAH?

God promised the nation of Israel that he would raise up a descendant from King David who would one day establish a righteous throne forever (see 2 Samuel 7:11-16). The Hebrew word *Messiah*, the equivalent of the Greek *Christ*, actually means "Anointed One." And it was this person who would usher in God's eternal kingdom on earth.

More than 400 years before Jesus was born there existed over 60 major Old Testament prophecies about this coming Messiah, made over hundreds of years. This is of great historical and spiritual significance, because it is the Messiah who Isaiah prophesied would one day

> remove the cloud of gloom, the shadow of death that hangs over the earth. He will swallow up death forever! The Sovereign LORD will wipe away all tears. He will remove forever all insults and mocking against his land and people. The LORD has spoken! (Isaiah 25:7-8).

THE EVIDENCE OF PROPHECY

Of course Jesus did claim to be the "Anointed One."* But do the prophesies of the Old Testament confirm that he was actually the Messiah? The answer is *yes*. It's as if God gave us a specific way to recognize who the "Anointed One" would be, through what has been called *Messianic* prophesies.

It seems impossible, but because of these prophecies, out of billions of people born over thousands of years we are able to pinpoint one person in history as the Messiah. It is as if God had an answer waiting for us when we asked, "How will we know who the Messiah is?" Imagine we are having a conversation with God as he uses these prophecies to pinpoint who this Messiah would be.

---

* See "Did Jesus Really Claim to Be God?" on page 109.

God begins by saying, "You will know he is the Messiah because I will cause him to be born as an Israelite, a descendent of Abraham" (Genesis 22:18; Galatians 3:16).

"But God," we protest, "Abraham's descendants will be many!"

"Then I will narrow it down to only half of Abraham's lineage and make him a descendant of Isaac, not Ishmael" (Genesis 21:12; Luke 3:23-34).

"That will help, but isn't that still an awful lot of people?"

"Let him be born from Jacob's line, then, eliminating half of Isaac's lineage" (Numbers 24:17; Luke 3:23-34).

"But—"

"I will be more specific. Jacob will have 12 sons; I will bring forth the Messiah from the tribe of Judah" (Genesis 49:10; Luke 3:23-33).

"Won't that still be a lot of people? Again, we may not recognize him when he comes."

"Don't worry! Look for him in the family line of Jesse" (Isaiah 11:1; Luke 3:23-32). "*And* from the house and lineage of Jesse's youngest son, David" (Jeremiah 23:5; Luke 3:23-31). "And then I will tell you *where* he will be born: Bethlehem, a tiny town in the area called Judah" (Micah 5:2; Matthew 2:1).

"But how will we know which person born there is the Messiah?"

"He will be preceded by a messenger who will prepare the way and announce his advent" (Isaiah 40:3; Matthew 3:1-2). "He will begin his ministry in Galilee" (Isaiah 9:1; Matthew 4:12-17) "and will teach in parables" (Psalm 78:2; Matthew 13:34-35), "performing many miracles" (Isaiah 35:5-6; Matthew 9:35).

"Okay, that should help a lot."

"Oh," God responds, "I'm just getting warmed up. He will ride into the city of Jerusalem on a donkey" (Zechariah 9:9; Matthew 21:2; Luke 19:35-37) "and will appear suddenly and forcefully at the temple courts and zealously 'clean house'" (Psalm 69:9; Malachi 3:1; John 2:15-16). "Why, in *one day* I will fulfill no fewer than *29* specific prophecies spoken at least 500 years earlier about him! Listen to this:

1. He will be betrayed by a friend (Psalm 41:9; Matthew 26:49).
2. The price of his betrayal will be 30 pieces of silver (Zechariah 11:12; Matthew 26:15).
3. The betrayal money will be cast to the floor of my temple (Zechariah 11:13; Matthew 27:5).

4. His betrayal money will be used to buy the potter's field (Zechariah 11:13; Matthew 27:7).

5. He will be forsaken and deserted by his disciples (Zechariah 13:7; Mark 14:50).

6. He will be accused by false witnesses (Psalm 35:11; Matthew 26:59-60).

7. He will be silent before his accusers (Isaiah 53:7; Matthew 27:12).

8. He will be wounded and bruised (Isaiah 53:5; Matthew 27:26).

9. He will be hated without a cause (Psalm 69:4; John 15:25).

10. He will be struck and spit on (Isaiah 50:6; Matthew 26:67).

11. He will be mocked, ridiculed, and rejected (Isaiah 53:3; Matthew 27:27-31).

12. He will collapse from weakness (Psalm 109:24-25; Luke 23:26).

13. He will be taunted with specific words (Psalm 22:6-8; Matthew 27:39-43).

14. People will shake their heads at him (Psalm 109:25; Matthew 27:39).

15. People will stare at him (Psalm 22:17; Luke 23:35).

16. He will be executed among 'sinners' (Isaiah 53:12; Matthew 27:38).

17. His hands and feet will be pierced (Psalm 22:16; Luke 23:33).

18. He will pray for his persecutors (Isaiah 53:12; Luke 23:34).

19. His friends and family will stand far off and watch (Psalm 38:11; Luke 23:49).

20. His garments will be divided up and awarded by the casting of lots (Psalm 22:18; John 19:23-24).

21. He will thirst (Psalm 69:21; John 19:28).

22. He will be given gall and vinegar (Psalm 69:21; Matthew 27:34).

23. He will commit himself to God (Psalm 31:5; Luke 23:46).

24. His bones will be left unbroken (Psalm 34:20; John 19:33).

25. His heart will rupture (Psalm 22:14; John 19:34).

26. His side will be pierced (Zechariah 12:10; John 19:34).

27. Darkness will come over the land at midday (Amos 8:9; Matthew 27:45).

28. He will be buried in a rich man's tomb (Isaiah 53:9; Matthew 27:57-60).

29. He will enter Jerusalem as a king 483 years after the declaration of Artaxerxes to rebuild the temple (444 BC) (Daniel 9:24).[33]

"As a final testimony, on the third day after his death, he will be raised from the dead" (Psalm 16:10; Acts 2:31), "ascend to heaven" (Psalm 68:18; Acts 1:9), "and be seated at my right hand in full majesty and authority" (Psalm 110:1; Hebrews 1:3).

———

As you can see, God has gone to extraordinary lengths to identify his Son Jesus as the Christ—the Messiah who would give his life for us. And one day, "when he has conquered all things, the Son will present himself to God, so that God, who gave his Son authority over all things, will be utterly supreme over everything everywhere" (1 Corinthians 15:28).

We can be confident that Jesus was the Messiah prophesied in Scripture. In fact, because there are 60 major Old Testament prophecies (with about 270 additional ramifications) fulfilled in one person named Jesus, we can be more than confident. The probability that all these prophecies were fulfilled in one person just by chance is overwhelmingly small.*

———

* To discover the probability factor and other details of Messianic prophecies, check out chapter 11 of *More Than a Carpenter*. For more information about *More Than a Carpenter*, see the back of this book.

43.

IS THERE PROOF THAT JESUS
WAS BORN OF A VIRGIN?

You don't have to know much about the "birds and the bees" to know that virgins don't have children by remaining virgins. Human reproduction requires that a female's ovum (egg) be fertilized by a male's gamete (sperm) to achieve human conception. There simply is no other option short of a miracle. So what proof is there that Jesus was miraculously born of a virgin?

Those who don't believe in miracles of course dismiss the virgin birth. In fact, Mary, Jesus' mother, questioned the whole concept herself when the angel Gabriel announced it to her. "Mary asked the angel, 'But how can this happen? I am a virgin'" (Luke 1:34). The angel explained that the conception would happen by the Holy Spirit, "so the baby to be born will be holy, and he will be called the Son of God" (Luke 1:35). The angel acknowledged that all this was miraculous and added, "Nothing is impossible with God" (Luke 1:37). God does perform miracles, and in this case he caused Mary's pregnancy.*

A MISTRANSLATION?

The prophet Isaiah foretold that Jesus would be born of a virgin seven centuries before the event took place. One objection that critics make is that the New Testament writer "misquotes" the word *virgin* from Isaiah 7. The Hebrew word used in Isaiah 7:14 is *'almah,* meaning "young woman." Yet the Gospel writer Matthew, quoting the Greek translation of the Old Testament, used the word *parthenos,* meaning "virgin." Critics say that Matthew is twisting what Isaiah was saying.

Truth is, the Hebrew word *'almah* can mean either "young woman" or "virgin," even though there is a specific word for *virgin* in Hebrew. However, because of the word's traditional usage, readers of Isaiah's time understood he did mean that a virgin would conceive. And that is why the

---

* See the paragraphs about miracles in "How Did Jesus Back Up His Claim to Be God?" on page 115.

Jewish scholars over 200 years before Jesus was born rendered the Hebrew word *'almah* as the Greek word for *virgin* when translating Isaiah 7:14 for the Septuagint. Matthew wasn't twisting things at all—he was quoting the Greek translation, considered both then and now to be accurate in translating Isaiah.

HOW PEOPLE REACTED

Prophecy provides clear evidence that Jesus was born of a virgin. But there is more. Notice how Scripture says that people of Jesus' hometown, Nazareth, reacted to him after he began his public ministry. On one occasion, after he had taught in the synagogue, the people he had grown up with said, "'He's just a carpenter, the son of Mary'...They were deeply offended and refused to believe in him" (Mark 6:3). The label "son of Mary" was an unambiguous insult in a society that called children by the name of their fathers—except, of course, in the case of children whose paternity was doubted.

At another time, Jesus' opponents threw a barb at him when they retorted, "*We* were not born out of wedlock!" (John 8:41). The insult and the reference to Jesus as the "son of Mary" and "born out of wedlock" indicate that it was common knowledge in Jesus' hometown that he had been conceived before Mary's wedding to Joseph—and without his aid. In other words, it seems very likely that the circumstances of Jesus' miraculous birth to a virgin caused him to be labeled as an illegitimate child.

Also, when Mary turned up pregnant, why would she have insisted she was a virgin? She knew that such a story would certainly be considered too wild to believe; why didn't she come up with something more credible? She could have concocted an excuse to make herself look innocent, or at least to put part of the blame on someone else. She could have claimed she was raped, or that Joseph had pressured her into yielding to his desire. He would have known better, but no one else would have. But instead of a rational explanation that would fit the known laws of nature, she told people she was pregnant by God's Holy Spirit. Why would she have said such a thing when it was the least believable of explanations? Only one reason makes sense. It was true.

And one final bit of evidence. When Mary turned up pregnant, what did Joseph, her fiancé, do? He naturally assumed she had had sex with another man and planned to call off the engagement and upcoming marriage. Matthew's account of the story, however, reports that an angel told

Joseph the truth about the conception. And based on that, he believed that Mary's child had been conceived by the Holy Spirit and went forward with the wedding.

Joseph made his decision fully aware of its implications. At first he did not believe Mary and resolved to break the engagement, just as any good man would do. It shows us he knew full well the implications of violating social expectations about purity and the sanctity of marriage. A good and prudent man, as Matthew calls him, would be very aware of how marrying Mary would mar his reputation for the rest of his life. So why did he go on and marry her? Only one reason makes any sense at all. He knew the truth. He believed the message from the angel and that it was the absolute truth. Mary was indeed a virgin who was bearing in her womb the Son of God conceived by the Holy Spirit.

44

IS THERE PROOF THAT JESUS ROSE FROM THE DEAD?

Once a person dies, really dies, and is buried, there is no coming back. People just don't rise from the dead naturally. It is impossible without miraculous intervention. So is there proof that a miracle took place—that Jesus was dead and then was bodily resurrected?

There is an abundance of evidence to support Jesus' resurrection. Many good resources are available on the subject.* However, there are also a number of alternative theories that try to explain the absence of Jesus' body from his tomb. They include the "stolen-body theory," "the relocated body theory," "the hallucination theory," "the spiritual resurrection theory," and others. Each of these theories attempts to explain facts about which there is little debate. The question is not whether those facts are true, but which theory best explains them. We will consider three of those facts.

FACT 1: JESUS DIED ON THE CROSS

The evidence for Jesus' death by crucifixion at the hands of the Romans is considerable:

1. All four Gospels report Jesus' death.

2. The nature of crucifixion virtually guaranteed death. Crucifixion had been methodically developed by the Romans to cause maximal pain over the longest possible time. Given Jesus' brutal whipping, the crown of thorns, the crossbar burden, and his being affixed to the cross with nails or spikes, it is virtually certain he was dead.

3. The spear thrust into Jesus' side, reported in the book of John, caused water and blood to flow out, which is medical evidence that Jesus died. Many physicians have agreed that

---

* We wrote our own book on the subject entitled *Evidence for the Resurrection* (Regal Books, 2009). Check it out for more details.

the release of blood and water from such a spear wound is a
sure sign of death.

4. Extrabiblical writers record the death of Jesus. These include
   Cornelius Tacitus (about AD 55–120), who is considered by
   many to be the greatest ancient Roman historian; the Jewish
   scholar Josephus (about AD 37–97); and the Jewish Talmud
   (compiled from about AD 70–200).

FACT 2: THE TOMB OF JESUS WAS EMPTY

On Sunday after the crucifixion, Mary and the other women went to
anoint the body of Jesus. To their surprise, the tomb was open and the
body was gone. There is good reason to believe the tomb was actually
empty as the women reported:

1. The disciples of Jesus did not go off to Egypt or China to
   preach the resurrection of Christ; they went right back to the
   city of Jerusalem, where Jesus was crucified. Had the tomb
   of Jesus been occupied, they could not have maintained the
   resurrection for a moment.

2. You can be sure that if Jesus' body hadn't been resurrected,
   the religious and political leaders of the day would have
   quickly and effectively quashed the rising sect of Christianity
   by locating the corpse and wheeling it through the streets of
   Jerusalem. This would have destroyed Christianity practically
   before it started. But this never happened, because Jesus had
   bodily risen from the dead.

3. One of the most compelling evidences supporting the empty
   tomb story is this: It reports that women first discovered the
   absence of Jesus' body. In first-century Palestine, women
   had low status as citizens or legal witnesses. Except in rare
   circumstances, Jewish law precluded women from giving
   testimony in a court of law. So why would the disciples,
   if they were contriving the story, have reported women
   as the first witnesses to the empty tomb? Typically when
   people concoct a story to deceive others, they don't invent
   information that discredits it. The fact that the disciples

include women as the first witnesses to the empty tomb
points to one thing—*they were reporting the truth.*

FACT 3: JESUS' DISCIPLES SINCERELY BELIEVED HE APPEARED TO THEM

Scholars agree that the early disciples sincerely believed that Jesus rose
from the dead and personally appeared to them. A convincing line of evidence can be found in 1 Corinthians 15:3-8, which is a short creed that
records the death, burial, resurrection, and appearances of Jesus to Peter,
James, the 12 disciples, a group of 500 believers, and finally to Paul.

Even though the book of 1 Corinthians was written around AD 55,
scholars believe the short creed in chapter 15 predates the writing of the
book itself. One reason is because at the beginning of the creed Paul says,
"I delivered to you as of first importance what I also received" (1 Corinthians 15:3 NASB). In other words, Paul is passing on to the Corinthian
church what had previously been given to him. When did Paul receive
the creed? Since Paul first visited Peter and James in Jerusalem three years
after his conversion (Galatians 1:18-20), many critical scholars believe that
Paul received the creed from them on this initial encounter. This would
date it to within five years after the death of Jesus. Historically speaking,
this is remarkably early evidence for belief in the death, burial, and appearances of Jesus.

Examine all the alternative theories, and only one conclusion takes
into account all the facts and does not adjust them to preconceived
notions. Christ's resurrection from the dead is a historical event caused by
a supernatural act of God.

45.

WHY DID JESUS NEED TO DIE?

T he Bible says we have all sinned (Romans 3:23) and are in need of forgiveness. But why did Jesus need to die to enable us to be forgiven by God? Isn't that an extreme measure for God to use in order to forgive people for making some bad choices?

SIN'S ROLE

To understand why Jesus had to die we must understand a little of what sin is and the nature of God.* We will summarize these two issues to place this question within a proper context.

God is a relational God who is by nature perfectly holy (Isaiah 54:5 and Revelation 4:8) and absolutely just (Revelation 16:5). Scripture says, "He is the Rock; his deeds are perfect. Everything he does is just and fair" (Deuteronomy 32:4). Doing holy and just things isn't something God decides to do, it is something he *is*. He by nature is holy and just.

Because he is perfectly holy by nature he can neither sin nor be in relationship with sin.† The Bible says of him, "Your eyes are too pure to look on evil; you cannot tolerate wrongdoing" (Habakkuk 1:13 NIV). So God is a pure and holy God that never does wrong, and that is a very good thing.

But as we stated, God is also just. "The LORD is just!" the Bible says. "He is my rock! There is no evil in him!" (Psalm 92:15). "All his acts are just and true" (Daniel 4:37). It is this just and holy God who recognizes evil for what it is and demands that sin be either eternally separated from him or paid for in a manner that absolves the guilt of it.

WHAT ABOUT HUMANS?

Now this is where we humans come in. The first human couple made a free choice to distrust God and disobey him. This resulted in sin, and sin resulted in the couple's separation from a perfect, holy God—that is called

---

* See "What Causes People to Sin Today?" on page 54 and "What Is God Really Like?" on page 39.

† See "If God Is So Loving Why Can't He Be More Tolerant of Sin?" on page 56.

death. So for Adam and Eve sin was a choice. But for all their offspring, sin and death became a condition. "When Adam sinned," the Scripture says, "sin entered the world. Adam's sin brought death, so death spread to everyone, for everyone sinned" (Romans 5:12).

So what was God to do? He couldn't have a relationship with humans as they were, because of sin—that would violate his holiness and purity. He couldn't overlook sin and say, "Oh, that's okay—I'll let bygones be bygones." That would violate his justice. But if he did nothing humans would remain eternally separated from him.

God's holiness couldn't abide sin and his justice couldn't overlook it. Yet his love couldn't stand by and do nothing. So he devised a masterful and merciful plan. But it would cost him dearly—the death of his only Son.

But why was Jesus' death required? Couldn't all of us simply perform some kind of penance to achieve our forgiveness and satisfy God's holiness and justice? Not in a million lifetimes! Why? Because we are all spiritually dead to God. Our sin condition has rendered us dead, and dead people can do nothing to remedy their condition.

That was the dilemma humans were in. That is why the Bible says, "When we were utterly helpless, Christ came at just the right time and died for us sinners" (Romans 5:6). No amount of good deeds on our part is acceptable to God, because we are dead to him. That is why only Jesus' death would do. He was the "sinless, spotless Lamb of God" (1 Peter 1:19). And when we place our faith in him "to take away our sins...God in his gracious kindness [grace] declares us not guilty" (Romans 3:22,24 NLT). "For God made Christ, who never sinned, to be the offering for our sin, so that we could be made right with God through Christ" (2 Corinthians 5:21).

There was no way for God's holiness and justice to be satisfied except for Jesus, God's sinless Son, to die for us. And because God's perfect justice was satisfied, Jesus could do the seemingly impossible—break the power of death over us. "Because God's children are human beings—" the Bible says, "made of flesh and blood—the Son also became flesh and blood. For only as a human being could he die, and only by dying could he break the power of the devil, who had the power of death" (Hebrews 2:14).

Jesus' death and resurrection was indispensable for us to be made right with a holy and just God. And because God wanted an eternal relationship with us so much he was willing to pay such a high price. And that is when Christ's eternal life becomes our inheritance, "for his Spirit joins with our spirit to affirm that we are God's children. And since we are his children, we are his heirs. In fact, together with Christ we are heirs of God's glory" (Romans 8:16-17).

46.

WHY IS JESUS' RESURRECTION SO CENTRAL TO CHRISTIANITY?

Some Christian leaders and pastors make the resurrection of Jesus central to Christianity. Others say of this that's it's almost as if such people believe that Jesus dying for our sins wasn't enough. And isn't Christ's death on the cross the central issue of Christianity, not his resurrection? Because it is Jesus' death that redeems us, right?

There is a reason Jesus' resurrection is so central to the Christian faith. It is not an optional article of faith—it is *the* faith! The resurrection of Jesus Christ and Christianity stand or fall together. One cannot be true without the other. Belief in the truth of Christianity is not merely faith in faith—ours or someone else's—but rather faith in the risen Christ of history. Without the historical resurrection of Jesus, the Christian faith is a mere placebo. The apostle Paul said, "If Christ has not been raised, then your faith is useless" (1 Corinthians 15:17). Worship, fellowship, Bible study, the Christian life, and the church itself are worthless exercises in futility if Jesus has not been literally and physically raised from the dead. Without the resurrection, we might as well forget God, church, and following moral rules and "feast and drink, for tomorrow we die!" (1 Corinthians 15:32).

On the other hand, if Christ has been raised from the dead, then he is alive at this very moment, and we can know him personally. The whole of 1 Corinthians 15:1-58 gives us assurance that our sins are forgiven (see verse 3) and that Christ has broken the power of death (see verse 54). Furthermore, he promises that we too will be resurrected someday (see verse 22). We can trust him because he is sovereign over the world (see verse 27). And he will give us ultimate victory (see verse 57), as well as a plan for our lives (see verse 58).

Christ's resurrection is therefore central to Christianity. Contemporary theologian J.I. Packer puts it this way:

> The Easter event...demonstrated Jesus' deity; validated his
> teaching; attested the completion of his work of atonement

for sin; confirms his present cosmic dominion and his coming reappearance as Judge; assures us that his personal pardon,
presence, and power in people's lives today is fact; and guar-
antees each believer's own re-embodiment by Resurrection in
the world to come.[34]

God is able to raise us to life in him because of the resurrected Jesus.
The power of his resurrection not only overcame his own death, but it will
one day defeat Satan and his hold of death on all of us:

> Christ must reign until he humbles all his enemies beneath
> his feet. And the last enemy to be destroyed is death...Then
> when he has conquered all things, the Son will present him-
> self to God, so that God, who gave his Son authority over all
> things, will be utterly supreme over everything everywhere
> (1 Corinthians 25-26,28 NLT).

47.

How Did People Get Right with God Before Jesus Died for Sin?

If trust in Christ's sacrificial death on the cross and his resurrection is what brings us into right relationship with God, then what about those who lived before Christ? Some people say that before him, obedience to the Old Testament law was what saved people, but after he came we are all saved by grace through faith in him. Other people say it was the sacrificial system of the Mosaic Law that saved people in that day. What is correct?

IT HAS ALWAYS BEEN BY GRACE THROUGH FAITH IN CHRIST

Actually, gaining forgiveness of sin and a right relationship with God was the same for those living before Christ as it is for those living after him. We are all made right with God by his grace through faith in his provision of salvation, namely his Son, Jesus.

From the very beginning God made faith in him the condition of a relationship with him. When God told Adam and Eve not to eat fruit from a certain tree, he was asking them to trust him. He wanted them to believe that his command was in their best interest and came from a God who cared for them. Down through the ages that has never changed. He has always wanted his human creation to believe that he loved them and to love and worship him in return.

So when humans sinned, God wasn't just wanting them to correct things by following his rules—or a sacrificial system—he wanted to restore a trusting relationship in which they worshipped him as their loving God. Obedience then becomes a natural by-product of that trusting and loving relationship. When King David sinned he prayed, "Purify me from my sins, and I will be clean; wash me, and I will be whiter than snow" (Psalm 51:7). David didn't see forgiveness coming by works or obedience, and he knew that sacrifices weren't what God was ultimately after. "You do not desire a sacrifice," David prayed, "or I would offer one. You do not want a burnt offering. The sacrifice you desire is a broken spirit. You will not reject a broken and repentant heart, O God" (Psalm 51:16-17).

Rather, David understood that a relationship with God was by God's grace as he placed his trust in him. "Protect me, for I am devoted to you. Save me, for I serve you and trust you. You are my God" (Psalm 86:2). Note that this doesn't mean Christ's death was unnecessary. It was indispensable to get us into a loving and trusting relationship with God.*

The apostle Paul expands on the matter of faith and explains how Abraham became right with God.

> If his [Abraham's] good deeds had made him acceptable to God, he would have had something to boast about. But that was not God's way. For the Scripture tells us, "Abraham believed God, and God counted him as righteous because of his faith"...People are counted as righteous, not because of their work, but because of their faith in God who forgives sinners. David also spoke of this when he described the happiness of those who are declared righteous without working for it: "Oh, what joy for those whose disobedience is forgiven, whose sins are put out of sight. Yes, what joy for those whose record the LORD has cleared of sins" (Romans 4:2-3,5-8).

Those living in Old Testament times sacrificed animals, but that was a temporary substitute that pointed to the Messiah who would sacrifice himself for them. "Jesus did this once for all," the Scripture states, "when he offered himself as the sacrifice for the people's sins" (Hebrews 7:27).

Just as Christ's death and resurrection reach forward in time to raise us from spiritual death into a right relationship with God, so they also reach back in time to deliver all those born before Jesus. The apostle Paul said that Jesus' "sacrifice shows that God was being fair when he held back and did not punish those who sinned in times past, for he was looking ahead and including them in what he would do in this present time" (Romans 3:25-26).

---

* See "Why Did Jesus Need to Die?" on page 127 and "Why Is Jesus' Resurrection So Central to Christianity?" on page 130.

In other words, those living prior to Jesus got credit for his sacrifice even before he died for them. It's like the case today when we buy something on credit—we get to use the merchandise or service even though, technically, we haven't paid for it yet. That is what the Scriptures mean when they say that Abraham "believed the LORD, and he credited it to him as righteousness" (Genesis 15:6 NIV). Abraham had salvation applied to him even though the final transaction by Jesus had not yet been completed. In sum, Jesus' perfect sacrifice solves the sin and death problem for all those who believe in God's provision—past, present, and future. All those who have died trusting in God's provision, all of us who are still living, and all those who will come after us must place faith in Christ's death and resurrection as their salvation and in his promise to one day raise us to life eternal.

48.

WHAT IS GOD'S CHURCH?

Some people today take issue with how churches function and with the various teachings coming out of the church. But where did the idea of the organized Christian religion come from? What do we really mean when we talk about "the church"?

Jesus asked his followers, "Who do you say that I am?" and Peter answered, "'You are the Messiah, the Son of the living God.' Jesus replied...'You are Peter (which means rock), and upon this rock I will build my church'" (Matthew 16:16-18). What kind of church did Jesus have in mind when he said this?

It was clear that when Jesus said *church,* he didn't mean a building. His word choice in the Greek was *ekklesia*, which meant a gathering of people. In the culture of that time the word *ekklesia* was clearly understood to mean a public assembly of citizens. Its Hebrew counterpart meant an assembly before the Lord. Whether in Greek or Hebrew, *church* meant "the people of God," not a building.

In today's culture, *church* is most often thought of as a building or an organization. But that is far from what the disciples and apostles understood after the Holy Spirit came on the day of Pentecost. Once the Holy Spirit filled them they understood the concept—the church was God's people. The church was Christ's agent to spread the kingdom message. The church was the visible representation of Christ himself.

When Jesus told his disciples to "go and make disciples of all the nations" (Matthew 28:19) he was delivering that command to his people, the church that would shortly be established. That church was given a mission, which was part of a greater mission of redemption and restoration of all things. Christ's initial step in that mission was to give his life as a ransom. He completed that through his death on the cross and his resurrection, but he would accomplish the rest of his mission through another means. With him as its head, the church would go viral—through the power of the Holy Spirit lived out in the community of his followers—and eventually every corner of the earth would be reached.

Jesus' new church wouldn't be a static organization, but a living organism. It wouldn't be about building an institution or a memorial, but about spreading a message and transforming the hearts of people. The New Testament uses at least six images to describe the church, none of which are about organizations, institutions, or physical buildings:

1. The church is the new people of God. (See Galatians 6:15-16 and Ephesians 3:10-11.)

2. The church is God's family. (See Ephesians 2:19-20 and Romans 8:14-17.)

3. The church is the Body of Christ. (See Ephesians 1:23 and Romans 12:4-5.)

4. The church is a holy temple where God lives. (See Ephesians 2:21-22 and 1 Corinthians 3:16.)

5. The church is Christ's pure bride. (See Ephesians 5:25-27.)

6. The church is Christ's agent to fulfill his mission to redeem the lost. (See 1 Peter 2:9 and 2 Corinthians 5:18-20.)[35]

When people are made right with God by grace through faith in Christ, they become part of this living community called the church.

49.

WHAT IS JESUS GOING TO DO
AT HIS SECOND COMING?

A lot of people have written about the Bible's prophecies about the last days and what is going to take place just before and after Jesus returns to earth. There are those who teach views called *premillennial*, *postmillennial*, and *amillennial*. And sometimes it can get rather confusing. But to get to the bottom line, what is Jesus really going to do when he returns the second time?

GOD'S RESTORATION PLAN

Jesus told his disciples that he was going away to prepare a place for them and for all who believe in him. And he gave this promise: "I will come again and receive you to Myself, that where I am, there you may be also" (John 14:3 NASB). After Pentecost, Peter preached this same message to the people of Jerusalem and said that Jesus "must remain in heaven until the time for the final restoration of all things, as God promised long ago through his holy prophets" (Acts 3:21). And what had the prophets said about God's restoration plans?

> "Look! I am creating new heavens and a new earth—and no one will even think about the old ones anymore" (Isaiah 65:17).

> The time will come when all the earth will be filled, as the waters fill the sea, with an awareness of the glory of the LORD (Habakkuk 2:14 NLT).

> "As the new heavens and the new earth that I make will endure before me," declares the LORD, "so will your name and descendants endure" (Isaiah 66:22 NIV).

These promises God declared were directed to the children of Israel, but they also include us as beneficiaries. When Peter asked what was in store for the disciples who followed Jesus, he was told, "At the renewal of all things, when the Son of Man sits on his glorious throne, you who have followed me will also sit on twelve thrones, judging the twelve tribes of Israel" (Matthew 19:28 NIV). Peter later wrote, "In keeping with his promise we are looking forward to a new heaven and a new earth, the home of righteousness" (2 Peter 3:13 NIV). Jesus also told us that "when the Son of Man comes in his glory," he "will say to those on his right, 'Come, you who are blessed by my Father; take your inheritance, the kingdom prepared for you since the creation of the world'" (Matthew 25:31,34 NIV).

God has not given up on his original plan. He has neither abandoned the idea of a perfect earth, nor has he laid aside his plan for his children to live in that perfect place forever. He has no intention of taking us away to some distant heaven and then destroying this earth he designed to be our home. After his resurrection, Jesus ascended into heaven with a promise to return. He will return and restore this earth to his original design. God's perfect plan is "to bring all things in heaven and on earth together under one head, even Christ" (Ephesians 1:10 NIV).

God will restore not only this earth to its original design, but our bodies as well. Our earthly bodies will be "transformed into heavenly bodies that will never die. When this happens...then at last the Scriptures will come true: 'Death is swallowed up in victory'" (1 Corinthians 15:53-54 NLT).

And all this, the restoration of our bodies and a new world, is dependent upon Jesus Christ returning to destroy death and, of course, his archenemy, the devil. Jesus first had to die as an atonement for our sin. And he did. He then had to conquer death through his resurrection to become our High Priest. And he did. And upon his second coming he will destroy death and the evil one to renew and restore all things.

> When he has conquered all things, the Son will present himself to God, so that God, who gave his Son authority over all things, will be utterly supreme over everything everywhere (1 Corinthians 15:28 NLT).[36]

50.

HOW DO I PERSONALLY EXPERIENCE A RELATIONSHIP WITH GOD?

There are a lot of questions we can have about God. And in this book we have attempted to answer 49 of them. But this one is really the most important: How do we experience a personal relationship with the living God?

He went to extraordinary lengths to form a relationship with you. He left heaven in the person of his Son, Jesus, died a terrible death, and rose again to raise you to new life in him. And he did all this because "he is a God who is passionate about his relationship with you" (Exodus 34:14).

Here is a simple presentation of the gospel story that you can use as a guide to establishing a relationship with God.

1. Can you really know God personally?

- God *loves* you. "This is real love—not that we loved God, but that he loved us" (1 John 4:10).

- God has a *plan* for you to know him personally. "This is eternal life: that they know you, the only true God, and Jesus Christ, whom you have sent" (John 17:3 NIV).

2. What prevents you from knowing God personally?

- Humans are sinful. "All have sinned and fall short of the glory of God" (Romans 3:23 NIV). Although we were created to have a relationship with God, because of our self-centeredness we choose to go our own independent way in disobedience to him. This self-will, characterized by an attitude of active rebellion or passive indifference, is an evidence of what the Bible calls sin.

- Humans are *separated*. "The wages of sin is death" (Romans

6:23). The death Paul speaks of here is not mere physical death, but spiritual separation from God. It means that "those who do not know God and do not obey the gospel of our Lord Jesus...will be punished with everlasting destruction and shut out from the presence of the Lord" (2 Thessalonians 1:8-9 NIV).

3. God provided a way to bridge this separation. Jesus Christ, God's Son, is God's *only* provision for our sin. Through him alone we can know God personally and experience his love.

- *Christ died in our place.* "God sent Jesus to take the punishment for our sins and to satisfy God's anger against us" (Romans 3:25 NLT).

- *Christ rose from the dead.* "Christ died for our sins...He was buried, and he was raised from the dead on the third day, just as the Scriptures said" (1 Corinthians 15:3-4).

- *Christ is the only way to God.* Jesus said, "I am the way, the truth, and the life. No one can come to the Father except through me" (John 14:6).

But...

4. It is not enough to just *know* these truths.

- We must individually *receive* Jesus Christ as Savior and Lord; then we can know God personally and experience his love. "To all who received him, to those who believed in his name, he gave the right to become children of God" (John 1:12 NIV).

- We receive Christ through faith, placing our trust in him and his power and authority. "It is by grace you have been saved, through faith—and this not from yourselves, it is the gift of God—not by works, so that no one can boast" (Ephesians 2:8-9 NIV).

- We receive Christ by accepting his personal invitation.

And...

5. When you receive Christ, you are changed.

- When you receive him by faith, as an act of your will, you experience a new life. "He died for everyone so that those who receive his new life will no longer live to please themselves. Instead, they will live for Christ" (2 Corinthians 5:15).

Just to agree intellectually that Jesus Christ is the Son of God and that he died on the cross for your sins does not qualify as faith. Faith requires a serious renouncing of one's previous ways and a trust in God to direct the future. Mere intellectual belief is not adequate to have Christ come into your life. Nor is it enough to have an emotional religious experience. Receiving Christ involves turning to God from self (repentance) and trusting Christ to come into your life to forgive you of your sins and to make you what he wants you to be.

6. The Bible promises eternal life to all who receive Christ.

- When we receive him, we are assured of eternal life in heaven and joy here on earth. "God has given us eternal life, and this life is in his Son. Whoever has the Son has life; whoever does not have the Son of God does not have life. I write these things to you who believe in the name of the Son of God so that you may know that you have eternal life" (1 John 5:11-13 NIV).

If you have not yet trusted in Christ by faith, you can do so right now. The words of the following prayer are not magical; they are simply a suggestion to enable you to express a sincere desire to turn from self to God:

> *"Lord Jesus, I believe that you are who you claimed to be, and I want to know you personally. Thank you for dying on the cross for my sins. I accept your forgiveness and place my trust in you as my Savior and Lord. Come into my heart and make me the person you created me to be. In Christ's name. Amen."* [37]

QUESTIONS
ABOUT
THE BIBLE

51.

WHERE DID THE BIBLE
COME FROM?

Today, the Bible, containing the Old Testament and New Testament, is the most widely circulated book in history. It has been translated into more than 2400 languages, and its distribution reaches into the billions. But where did this extraordinary book come from? Who wrote it and when?

THE OLD TESTAMENT

The Old Testament portion of the Bible was written in the Hebrew language, except for a few passages that were written in Aramaic. It was written over a period of about a thousand years. The first person the Bible identifies as its writer is Moses. He is credited with authoring all of its first five books. The date of Moses' writing is considered to be during what is known as the late Bronze Age (1500s–1200s BC). The accounts of creation, Noah and the flood, Abraham's journeys, and so on were likely passed down orally from one generation to another. It is also possible that hundreds of years before Moses, Abraham may have written down what his great-great-grandfathers knew about the early stories of creation. But it was Moses who compiled those early narratives.

The entire Old Testament today is comprised of 39 books: the 5 books of Moses (known as the Pentateuch), 12 historical books, 5 books of poetry, and the 17 books of the major and minor prophets. While it is clear who wrote many of the books of the Old Testament, other books simply don't tell us.

THE NEW TESTAMENT

The New Testament wasn't written until after Jesus died, rose again, and ascended into heaven. During his time, the Jewish territories were primarily under the rule of the Romans and the descendants of Herod the Great. Greek and Aramaic were the primary languages. Most scholars estimate that the first writings of the New Testament were penned in Greek by the apostle Paul about 20 years after Jesus' resurrection and ascension. Paul is credited with writing most of the New Testament epistles. The four Gospels (Matthew, Mark, Luke, and John) are anonymous and do not name their authors. But the early Church Fathers were nearly unanimous that the apostles whose names are borne by the Gospels were in fact their authors. These accounts are believed to have been written between AD 65 and 90, but there is some evidence they may have been written earlier. The New Testament includes 27 books in all.

The materials used to write in early times included

- clay (Ezekiel 4:1)
- stone (Exodus 24:12)
- metal (Exodus 28:36)
- papyrus, which was two layers of split papyrus reeds pressed together to form a papery sheet (Revelation 5:1)
- vellum, made from calfskin; parchment, from lambskin; or leather, from cowhide (2 Timothy 4:13)

At some point each writing of Scripture had to be copied from the author's original medium in order to preserve it for future generations. Ink would fade, leather and parchment would decay, and papyrus would crumble. This called for individuals to carefully transcribe the original writing, called the *autographon* (plural, *autographa*), into an accurate copy known as a manuscript. The process of making copies from previous copies preserved the writings we now know as the Scripture.*

While we may have identified something of how we got the Bible we have today, the question remains: "Where did the words of the Bible come from?" The New Testament tells us clearly:

> Long ago God spoke many times and in many ways to our ancestors through the prophets. And now in these final days, he has spoken to us through his Son (Hebrews 1:1-2).

---

* See "Is the Old Testament Historically Reliable?" on page 192 and "Is the New Testament Historically Reliable?" on page 196.

"All Scripture is inspired by God and is useful to teach us…correct us… to prepare and equip his people" (2 Timothy 3:16-17). "You must realize that no prophecy in Scripture ever came from the prophets' own understanding, or from human initiative. No, those prophets were moved by the Holy Spirit and they spoke from God" (2 Peter 1:20-21). So the Bible actually comes from God. They are his words put in writing. A select group of men (known as prophets and apostles) wrote the Scriptures as they were guided and inspired by God.

The Almighty Creator God spoke verbally to the children of Israel from Mount Sinai just over three millennia ago (see Exodus 31:18). Then over the centuries he inspired more than 40 different prophets and apostles to write down his words to us. These authors were from every walk of life—shepherds, soldiers, prophets, poets, monarchs, scholars, statesmen, masters, servants, tax collectors, fishermen, and tentmakers. His Word was written in a variety of places: in the wilderness, in a palace, in a dungeon, on a hillside, in a prison, and in exile. It was penned on the continents of Asia, Africa, and Europe. It is written in a variety of genres, including biographies, narratives, poetry, law, letters, and more. With all its variety of authors, origins, and content, it achieves a remarkable purpose: It communicates to finite humans the very mind and heart of an infinite God.

52.

WHAT DOES IT MEAN THAT
THE BIBLE IS INSPIRED?

Have you ever been inspired to write a poem or a song? Have you ever been inspired by a parent, coach, or public speaker? Poems, novels, music, movies, and speakers can give us inspiration. When people say the Bible is inspired, is that what they mean—that the words of the Bible are inspirational?

GOD'S COMMUNICATION

When the apostle Paul said that "all Scripture is inspired by God" (2 Timothy 3:16), he did not mean that the Bible was merely an inspirational book. He used a specific word in the Greek language—*theopneustos*, which literally means "God-breathed" (*theos*, God; *pneō*, to breathe). All of Scripture is "God-breathed," which means the written words in the Bible are from God. That is why we refer to Scripture as the Word of God.

Jesus referred to Scripture this way when he told the Pharisees that they were misusing scriptural teaching. He said, "So you cancel the word of God [Scripture] for the sake of your own tradition" (Matthew 15:6). The apostle Paul explained how the Jewish people "have been entrusted with the very words of God" (Romans 3:2 NIV). So when you read the Bible you are not simply reading an inspirational book; you are reading words from God.

While Scripture is God's Word, it doesn't mean that God penned the words himself or put people into a trance and used their hands and pens to write out his thoughts and ideas. Rather, he chose people who had a spiritual relationship with him to be his spokesmen. And God spoke through them to write down his words and message through their unique personalities.

God spoke directly to Moses, and Moses relayed God's Word to the children of Israel verbally and in writing (see Exodus 19, 20, and 24). Later he told Israel that "the LORD your God will raise up for you a prophet like me...The LORD said to me...'I will put my words in his mouth, and he will tell the people everything I command him'" (Deuteronomy 18:15,17-18).

While some prophets heard audibly from God, others received God's words through dreams (Genesis 37:1-11), in a burning bush (Exodus), visions (Daniel 7 and Revelation 1:1-2), from angels (Genesis 19:1-29), or through an inner voice as "the word of the LORD that came to Hosea" and "to Joel" (Hosea 1:1 NLT and Joel 1:1), and so on.

So when it is said that Scripture is inspired by God it means he superintended what he wanted to be said through men as his instruments. The apostle Paul said, "When we tell you these things, we do not use words that come from human wisdom. Instead, we speak words given to us by the Spirit, using the Spirit's words to explain spiritual truths" (1 Corinthians 2:13). The apostle Peter made the same point when he wrote that "no prophecy in Scripture ever came from the prophet's own understanding, or from human initiative. No, those prophets were moved by the Holy Spirit and they spoke from God" (2 Peter 1:20-21).

Over 3000 times the biblical writers claimed to have received their words from God, using phrases like "the word of the LORD came to me" (Ezekiel), "the LORD said to Moses" (Leviticus), "says the LORD" (Isaiah), "declares the LORD" (Jeremiah), and so on. The apostle Paul said, "I want you to understand that the gospel message I preach is not based on mere human reasoning. I received my message from no human source, and no one taught me. Instead, I received it by direct revelation from Jesus Christ" (Galatians 1:11-12).

God's Word spoken and written by his prophets and apostles is a special revelation. Scripture was inspired by him so he could reveal his thoughts, words, and promises in order that we could have them preserved from generation to generation. So the Bible is a special revelation of God, written by human authors who were inspired directly by him. And because of that the Bible carries power and weight, or what we might call authority. Behind the Scripture stands the Sovereign God of the universe. And when he speaks, his Word defines the essence of authority.

God took special care over thousands of years to reveal his Word to select individuals who would carefully write down his thoughts and message. And he superintended that process so that what he wanted to have written was in fact written. And we have that permanent record in Scripture. As Jesus said,

"I tell you the truth, until heaven and earth disappear, not even the smallest detail of God's law will disappear until its purpose is achieved" (Matthew 5:18). Nothing will stamp out God's Word and nothing will impede his ultimate purpose. "Heaven and earth will disappear," Jesus said, "but my words will remain forever" (Matthew 24:35).

53.

IS THE BIBLE A PRODUCT OF GOD, HUMANS, OR BOTH?

The Bible is said to be God's Word—inspired by God or "God-breathed." So was the Bible dictated by him word-for-word to a select group of men—as if he were miraculously guiding their pens to write out his words?* Or perhaps he gave certain men some inspirational thoughts and gave them freedom to write their own interpretation of his message. Which is it?

GOD'S MEANS

As we covered in the previous question, the Bible is God's Word "breathed out" or spoken through his spokesmen. But the 40-some authors of the 66 books of the Bible were not mindless dictation machines, so to speak. God selected specific human authors with various backgrounds, different talents, select educational training, and varied life experiences for a very good reason. He, being infinite, wanted his Word to communicate clearly to finite humans. So he transmitted his thoughts and words through different humans with different personalities, styles, and voices. He chose shepherds, soldiers, prophets, poets, monarchs, scholars, servants, tax collectors, fishermen, and tentmakers because each had a unique human experience enabling them to convey a tapestry of meanings we could all understand.

It's as if God was composing a musical masterpiece using a 40-piece orchestra. Think of a Master Maestro who has created a specific musical composition. He uses different instruments for different purposes: the various drums set the rhythm, the trumpets call us to action, the violins and cellos soothe us, the flutes lift our spirits, and so on. In the hands of the Maestro the different and varied instruments produce a symphony of sounds that move the mind, heart, and emotions of the hearer with the message of the music. In a similar way, God used the different authors to

---

* See "What Does It Mean that the Bible Is Inspired?" on page 148.

impart his message clearly to us, no matter who we are or how varied our human experience might be.

GOD'S SERVANTS

Take the life experiences of King David. He started out as a shepherd, killed a giant, was a musician, had his life threatened by Saul, became king, committed adultery, fought and won wars, and so on. David knew what it meant to have ups and downs in life, and God used his multifaceted human experiences to powerfully communicate his Word...using David's tender heart of devotion, his desire to serve, his failings and sin, and his deep passion to know God intimately. There was King Solomon, gifted with insight and wisdom God chose to speak through. The prophet Hosea had an unhappy marriage to an unfaithful wife. God spoke through his life experiences to illustrate the unfaithfulness of Israel and God's unfailing and faithful love to his people.

The outspoken and overconfident disciple Peter actually denied Jesus. Yet in Peter's first letter (the book of 1 Peter) we have one of the greatest messages ever written on how to maintain a life of devotion and holiness in the midst of temptation and suffering. As with multiple musical instruments in an orchestra, God made use of the many and varied human experiences of his spokesmen to craft what he wanted us to know in words that would enable us to clearly understand his heart and mind.

Not only did God speak through spokesmen with varied human experiences, he also expressed his Word in a number of literary styles and forms. At times, the Bible reads like a novel, and at other times like a book of rules and regulations. The Scripture moves from the mournful laments of Jeremiah to the exalted poetry of Isaiah and the Psalms. The Bible uses this wide range of literary forms to communicate clearly to its human audience. God's Word is full of narratives, parables, allegories, metaphors, similes, satire, and hyperbole.

———

Because God spoke his words through humans, the Scripture is textured with varied literary forms and styles and the different human perspectives, emotions, and cultures of his spokesmen. In so communicating, God captures the full character of those he spoke through, from the tight-knit logic of a scholar (Paul, in his epistles) to the priestly perspective of a theologian (the writer of Hebrews) to the poetic talents of a musician (David in the Psalms) to the despair and agony of a people (Jeremiah in Lamentations). Each book of Scripture is presented through the lens of its human spokesman yet still conveys the exact message God wants us to receive.

So in one respect, we can say the Bible is a product of both God and humans. Yet its writing was supernaturally guided and divinely superintended to convey precisely what God wants to communicate. Therefore, it is rightly called the Word of God.

54

ISN'T THE BIBLE FULL OF ERRORS
AND CONTRADICTIONS?

The Bible contains 66 books authored by over 40 different people writing on hundreds of subjects, including who God is and how he interacts with his creation. Could all these different authors, who wrote hundreds of years apart, be consistent and in harmony regarding its message? Critics claim that is impossible and assert there are thousands of errors and contradictions in the Bible. Is this true?

When conservative Christian theologians say the Bible is without error (inerrant) they mean that, when all the facts are known, the Scriptures as they were penned by the authors in the original writings and as properly interpreted will be shown to be true and not false in all they affirm. This is of course the case if God is actually the author of Scripture.* It stands to reason that if he inspired certain men to reveal his words, he would be sure not to contradict himself, so that his Word would be error-free.

APPARENT PROBLEMS

So can anyone find errors and contradictions in the Bible? There may be *apparent* contradictions, but we contend there are no *actual* errors or contradictions in the original writings, called autographs. But those autographs no longer exist. What we have are copies of what was originally penned. In fact, we have thousands of copies.

Because there were no printing presses at the time Scripture was being written (nor were there any for more than another thousand years), men had to handwrite copies to preserve the documents from one generation to another. And while those who made the copies (scribes) did their best to copy accurately, some errors were made.† But just because there were copying mistakes does not mean the Bible is full of contradictions and errors. Because when you examine the "errors" it is clear how they were made and that they do not alter the intended meaning of the text.

---

* See "What Does It Mean that the Bible Is Inspired?" on page 148.

† See "Is the Old Testament Historically Reliable?" on page 192 and "Is the New Testament Historically Reliable?" on page 196.

For example, some manuscripts of the New Testament spell the name John with one "n"; other times it is spelled with two. This technically constitutes an error or contradiction. And whenever a particular "error" like this occurs, say in 3000 manuscripts, it counts as 3000 "errors." But of course that type of "error" in no way changes the meaning of God's Word.

Other errors can be found in both the Old and New Testaments, such as these:

- In 2 Chronicles 9:25 some manuscripts read that Solomon had 4000 horse stalls for the 14,000 chariots he owned. But in 1 Kings 4:26 other manuscripts say "40,000 horse stalls." Clearly Solomon didn't need 40,000 stalls to accommodate 14,000 chariots. This was obviously the result of an overworked and perhaps sleepy scribe copying down 40 instead of 4. This is an understandable human error.

- In 2 Chronicles 22:2, most manuscripts say that King Ahaziah was 22 years old. But in 2 Kings 8:26 some manuscripts report that he was 42. Of course he couldn't have been 42 or he would have been older than his father. Again, this was a copying error.

- In Matthew 28:2-3 it is reported that there was an angel at Jesus' tomb. But Luke 24:4 refers to two angels being there. Is this a contradiction? It's no more a contradiction than if I (Sean) report to you that I went to Disneyland last year. And then someone else tells you that my wife, Stephanie, and our two children went with me too. The first statement may have left you with the impression I went to the theme park alone, while the other report explains others were with me. But this is not a contradiction.

- Some have made an issue of Jesus saying he would be killed and would rise from the dead in three days (Mark 8:31). Technically, Jesus wasn't in the grave for three 24-hour days. Did he err in what he said? No, because in the Jewish culture any part of a day was considered a whole day. There was no contradiction here.

THE ACCURACY OF THE BIBLE'S TRANSMISSION

Because we are dealing only with copies of the original manuscripts and not the originals themselves, we are bound to have some copying errors. And it stands to reason that those copies that are closer to the originals are more likely to have fewer copying errors. Because if one error is made in copying down a manuscript, future manuscript copies are going to reproduce that error. So the earlier manuscripts tend to be more accurate because they are closer to the original. And we didn't know just how amazingly accurate the Old Testament copies were until the discovery of the Dead Sea Scrolls in 1947.

Before 1947, the oldest complete Hebrew manuscript dated to AD 900. But with the discovery of 223 manuscripts in caves on the west side of the Dead Sea, we came into possession of Old Testament manuscripts dated by paleographers to around 125 BC. These scrolls were a thousand years older than any previously known manuscripts.

But here's the exciting part: Once the Dead Sea Scrolls were compared with later manuscript copies, the then-current Hebrew Bible proved to be identical, word for word, in more than 95 percent of the text. The other 5 percent consisted mainly of spelling variations. For example, of the 166 words in Isaiah 53, only 17 letters were in question. Of those, 10 letters were a matter of spelling, and 4 were stylistic changes; the remaining 3 letters comprised the word *light*, which was added in verse 11.

In other words, the greatest manuscript discovery of all time revealed that a thousand years of copying the Old Testament had produced only very minor variations, none of which altered the clear meaning of the text or brought the manuscript's fundamental integrity into question.[38]

If there are apparent errors or contradictions in copied manuscripts of the Scriptures, three principles or ground rules should be used to investigate:*

1. Approach the Scriptures in the same way as other ancient literature, giving the benefit of the doubt to the document itself rather than the critic.

2. Exercise an open mind.

3. Submit to external, objective controls.

---

* Details of these principles are found in chapter 18 of *The New Evidence That Demands a Verdict*. For more information about *The New Evidence that Demands a Verdict*, see the back of this book.

55.

Does the New Testament Misquote the Old Testament?

The 39 books of the Old Testament were written to and about the children of Israel, or the Jewish nation. Some critics charge that writers of the New Testament twist Old Testament passages and take them out of context to make them fit their views of Jesus and his teachings. What are these purported distortions that critics refer to?

For example:

- Matthew quotes Isaiah 7 and declares that it was prophesied Jesus was to be born of a virgin and would be called Immanuel (Matthew 7:14). Critics point out that a full reading of chapter 7 of Isaiah shows it is more likely referring to the birth of Hezekiah, who became a godly king of Israel.

- Hosea the prophet says when Israel was a child, God loved him and "called my son out of Egypt" (Hosea 11:1). We all know that God did in fact call his people out of Egypt. Yet Matthew says this was a prophecy about Joseph and Mary taking Jesus to Egypt and their later return. They did this to escape Herod's decree to kill all the newborn Jewish males in Bethlehem.

- And then the critics say that Matthew quotes Jeremiah about Rachel weeping over her dead children. Yet the New Testament writer claims this was referring to first-century mothers weeping after Herod ordered the infant boys in Bethlehem to be killed.

Writers of the New Testament are accused of twisting and taking Old Testament passages like this out of context to teach their brand of Christianity. The writers of the Gospels and epistles seem to take liberties with the Old Testament text in order to establish a whole new religion of their own. Is this true?

GOD'S ULTIMATE CONTEXT

What the critics overlook is that Jesus came to fulfill God's promise to Israel and provide a means for all of his lost children to be redeemed. This means that many of the prophecies and promises to Israel were foreshadows of Jesus' plan to bring Israel and his church into his eternal kingdom.

Jesus came to establish his kingdom, and it was he who said, "Don't misunderstand why I have come. I did not come to abolish the law of Moses or the writings of the prophets. No, I came to accomplish their purpose" (Matthew 5:17). He was the realization of all the prophets and the law taught. He was the fulfillment of God's message to Israel, and therefore we must understand the Old Testament in light of him.

So Matthew and other writers of the New Testament weren't twisting the Old Testament passages or taking them out of context. Rather, they were understanding them as God had inspired his writers to understand them—Israel was God's means of bringing salvation to the world, and Jesus was the literal fulfillment of his masterful and merciful plan. Jesus was the true Son called out of Egypt that Israel failed to be. This was not a misinterpretation of Hosea 11:1. Isaiah did predict a child would be born to deliver Israel. Hezekiah was only a temporary salvation to God's people. God revealed through Matthew that Jesus was the permanent salvation not only for Israel but for the whole world.

Once Jesus ascended into heaven and sent his Holy Spirit, he opened the minds and hearts of his band of Jewish followers. And they saw that he was the embodiment or completer of the Old Testament events and images God had given them so many years before.

The apostles were empowered by the Holy Spirit with God-breathed words to reveal his plan, which was formed even before the foundations of the world. The apostle Paul said,

> God himself revealed his mysterious plan to me...God did not reveal it to previous generations, but now by his Spirit he has revealed it to his holy apostles and prophets. And this is God's plan: Both Gentiles and Jews who believe the Good News share equally in the riches inherited by God's children (Ephesians 3:3,5-6).

The New Testament writers did not misquote the Old Testament passages—they simply gave them the context centered on Christ that God intended.

56.

HOW DO WE KNOW THAT THE BIBLE WE HAVE TODAY IS TRULY GOD'S WORD?

Today our complete Bible is comprised of 39 books of the Old Testament and 27 books of the New Testament. But how do we know those are the God-inspired books God prepared for us? Who decided which books would be part of the Bible? Maybe some God-inspired books were overlooked. How do we know we have all the writings that were inspired by God?*

THE PROCESS OF THE CANON

Determining what writings were inspired by God (God-breathed) was not a specific event, but rather a process over time. It took some time to recognize which writings were God-inspired and to establish a process to know for sure which books were his Word. The 66 books accepted as God's inspired word are referred to as the *canon* of Scripture. *Canon* comes from the Greek word *kanōn,* meaning "rule" or "principle." In other words there was a very high standard or measuring tool needed to deem a writing "inspired by God."

Contrary to what some modern critics say, early Jewish and church leaders did not create the canon. In other words, a group of religious leaders did not determine which books would be called Scripture, the inspired Word of God. Rather, those leaders merely recognized or discovered which books were "God-breathed" from their very inception. That is to say, a writing was not given the authority of being Scripture because the early Jewish or Christian leaders accepted it as such. Instead, it was accepted by the leaders and the people because it was clear to them that God himself had given the writing its divine authority.

GUIDING PRINCIPLES FOR RECOGNITION

From what we find in biblical and church history we can see at least

---

* See "What Does It Mean that the Bible Is Inspired?" on page 148.

four guiding principles or rules that qualified a letter or book to be recognized as a divinely inspired writing.

1. The writing was authored by a prophet or apostle of God or someone connected with them.

2. The message of the book was consistent with what had already been revealed about God.

3. The writing clearly evidenced the confirming presence of God.

4. The book was widely accepted by the church from an early date.[39]

By as early as the 300s BC, and certainly no later than 150 BC, all the 39 books of the Old Testament had been written, collected, and officially recognized as canonical books.[40] The Hebrew text of these 39 books was originally divided into 24 books: 5 books of the Law (of Moses), 8 Prophets, and 11 Writings.

There could be no higher authority given to the Old Testament than that of Jesus himself. He repeatedly quoted and taught from it. On one occasion he stated, "that everything written about me in the law of Moses [the five books] and the prophets [the eight books] and in the Psalms [included in the eleven writings] must be fulfilled" (Luke 24:44). To further confirm his acceptance of the entire Old Testament canon, Jesus made reference to the first and last martyrs within its text when he said "from the murder of Abel to the murder of Zechariah" (Luke 11:51). He was referring to the entire span, from the first book, Genesis, to Chronicles, which was the final book in the Hebrew sequence of the Old Testament. (Since we have today reordered the 24 books of the Hebrew text and have divided them into 39, it was like Jesus saying "from Genesis to Malachi.") Clearly Jesus confirmed the authority and inspiration of the Hebrew canon.

Soon after Paul wrote his epistles they were recognized by the early church as inspired by God. The apostle Peter recognized this and indicated in 2 Peter 3:15-16 that he considered the letters of Paul to belong in the category of Scripture. Church Fathers of the first and second centuries, such as Clement of Alexandria, Ignatius, and Polycarp also recognized the authority of the writings that comprise our New Testament.

By the 200s and 300s, church elders began to set criteria for recognizing writings of the apostles as inspired by God. In AD 367, Athanasius of Alexandria provided the first official list of the 27 books of the New Testament we have today. And by the late 300s there was consensus. All 27 books were canonized by the councils of Hippo (AD 393) and Carthage (AD 397). Remember, this was not a group of church elders authorizing a collection of religious writings—rather, they were recognizing that this collection of books was authorized by God.

Of course there were numerous other letters, writings, and books circulated within the Jewish community and early church. But they were not recognized as Scripture. Why were they not included in our Bible? And why aren't we still adding spiritual writings to our Bible today? This will be covered in the next question.

57

Were Some Inspired Books Excluded from Our Current Bible?

Over 100 years before Christ was born, all 39 books of the Old Testament had been written, collected, and officially recognized as God's inspired Scripture (canonized) by the Jewish leaders. By the late 300s the 27 books of the New Testament were recognized as God-inspired.* But were there some good spiritual writings that were perhaps God-inspired but were overlooked or excluded from the official Bible? If so, why? And why isn't God still inspiring people to write his Word today?

WHAT IS "INSPIRATION"?

There are many people throughout history who have written spiritually inspiring books and letters. But there is good reason they are not considered equal to Scripture. And it is true that the Holy Spirit is alive today and does guide people to write inspiring literature. But Jewish and church leaders long ago concluded that the period of what is called God's special revelation and inspiration is past.

God spoke directly through his Old Testament prophets in times past to reveal himself. The New Testament writer of the book of Hebrews said, "Long ago God spoke many times and in many ways to our ancestors through the prophets. And now in these final days, he has spoken to us through his Son" (Hebrews 1:1-2). And once God delivered his complete message through his prophets he "closed the book" on the Old Testament. By as early as the 300s BC, all the 39 books of the Old Testament were considered to be the complete revelation of God to the Jewish people.

Jesus confirmed the completeness and authority of the entire Hebrew Scriptures (the 39 books of our current Old Testament) when he said that "everything written about me in the law of Moses and the prophets and in the Psalms must be fulfilled" (Luke 24:44). Jesus was referring to the entire Hebrew Old Testament. Nor did he ever cite any books other than the

---

* See "How Do We Know the Bible We Have Today Is Truly God's Word?" on page 159.

current 39 books of the Old Testament to indicate there was any other literature that was also God-inspired. And by using the phrase "all the Scriptures" (Luke 24:27 NLT) in regard to the Old Testament he showed that he accepted the same completed Jewish canon as did Judaism at that time.

The New Testament centers around the revelation of God through his Son, Jesus Christ, as written by his apostles. Obviously the best and most accurate writing about Jesus and all he revealed would be done by those who were in direct contact with him. Thus the men inspired by God to reveal the truth about his Son and his message would either be eyewitnesses or would know those who had personally heard the message of the gospel. By the end of the first century it became clear to the early church that God's special revelation and inspiration of Scripture was complete.

So the "inspiration" God gives writers today is not a special revelation of himself, but a reflection of what has been given in inspired Scripture. By comparing what people write and teach today with Scripture, we can know if it is in fact the truth of God.

THE APOCRYPHA

Yet early on there were some writings that emerged that some thought might be "God-breathed" Scripture. After the Old Testament canon had been recognized by Jewish leaders and officially closed, certain literature of a spiritual nature remained or appeared. Today these writings are referred to as the *Apocrypha*, which means "that which is hidden."

There were 14 books that some people added to the 39 canonized books in the Greek Septuagint translation of the Old Testament. These 14 books—the Apocrypha—were not accepted by the early church, but they were eventually included in the Old Testament by the Roman Catholic Church in AD 1546.*

These added books surfaced between about 200 BC into the second century AD.† They are

- First Esdras
- Second Esdras
- Tobit
- Judith

---

* See "How Is the Roman Catholic Bible Different from the Protestant Bible?" on page 209.

† For more details on these 14 books see chapter 2 of *More Evidence that Demands a Verdict*.

- Additions to Esther
- The Wisdom of Solomon
- Ecclesiasticus
- Baruch
- Susanna
- Bel and the Dragon (additions to Daniel)
- The Song of the Three Hebrew Children (additions to Daniel)
- The Prayer of Manasseh
- First Maccabees
- Second Maccabees

The books of the Apocrypha are not part of the Protestant Bible today for good reasons. For example, none of the 14 books of the Old Testament Apocrypha claimed divine inspiration—in fact some actually disclaimed it. Various credible historians, philosophers, and translators such as Josephus, Philo, and Jerome rejected them. They were never quoted as Scripture in the New Testament. And the early Church Fathers excluded them entirely.

THE CASE OF THE NEW TESTAMENT

What about the New Testament—were there certain letters or books that some considered Scripture but were excluded? By the end of the first century Paul's epistles and the four Gospels were widely accepted by the new Christian church as divinely inspired. Peter even wrote around AD 65 that all of Paul's known writings belonged in the category of Scripture (see 2 Peter 3:15-16). But by the middle of the second century there were a growing number of other writings that gained attention, and some wondered if they too were God-inspired. These became known as New Testament apocrypha and Gnostic writings (*Gnostic* meaning having to do with knowledge).

However, the Gnostic writings were rejected by the early church because they largely contradicted the Gospels and epistles of Paul. Some of these included *The Infancy Gospel of Thomas, The Gospel of Judas, The Gospel of Peter,* and *The Gospel of Thomas.* These writings taught that there were multiple creators; that ignorance was the ultimate problem—not sin; and that salvation was by "spiritual knowledge" for only a few. One Gnostic writing depicts a young Jesus striking other children down for bumping into him.

So by the late 300s, when the Church Fathers had established a clear means to recognize the authoritative Word of God, these works had been long rejected. In AD 367 Athanasius of Alexandria offered the first official list of the 27 books of the New Testament we have today. And by AD 397 the church councils of Hippo and Carthage accepted them as well.

58

How Can Teachings from the Ancient Cultures of the Bible Be Relevant to Us Today?

Let's face it, the Bible was written in a time and place vastly different from twenty-first-century North America. The customs, traditions, and overall culture were nowhere near ours today. What they were facing and how they dealt with issues of life simply don't relate to us. So how can the teachings of the Bible be relevant to modern society?

It is true the Old Testament was written from 2500 to over 3000 years ago. The New Testament was written roughly 2000 years ago. The cultures were different; there is no question about that. What people did and how they expressed themselves don't resemble much of our modern world.

It is also true that the New Testament, for example, commanded that men greet their Christian brothers with a "holy kiss." It instructed slave owners on how to treat their slaves and how slaves should respond to their masters. During biblical times daughters were given away to a man in arranged marriages, and wives had no legal rights.

But with all these cultural differences, the Bible is still extremely relevant to us today. That is because of what it is all about at its core.

A RELATIONAL REVELATION

The Bible is a revelation of God to mankind, which includes us. It explains who he is, what he is like, how he is passionate about a relationship with us, who we are, why we are here, why we are separated from him, and how we can regain a relationship with him. The Bible presents a view of life very different from how we humans see it. It presents God's view of the world—his worldview, to be exact. (A *worldview* is what we assume to be true about the basic makeup of our world.) And it is his worldview that God wants us to embrace.

God's Word gets at the deep level of a person's worldview. That is where beliefs are formed, values established, and relationships with God and others defined. It is at this level that choices are made. The Hebrew text and all of Jesus' teachings address this worldview level. The culture then isn't at issue, but rather how humans respond to God's worldview message. Scripture is getting at the individual choice to have a relationship with God, embrace his worldview, and live that out within a person's environment and circumstances. That makes the Bible relevant to any culture.

Because the Bible is all about a relationship with God and living out his worldview, it is cross-cultural. The truth about God and the reality of this world he has made is universal, and it is relevant to every person in every culture in every time period. Ultimately then, a Bible reader's goal should be to understand what God is saying to him or her personally—how Scripture is relevant and applicable to life in his or her present world.

HISTORICAL CONTEXT

To interpret and understand the relevancy of Scripture to our lives involves a two-step process. The first step is *to determine what the specific passages meant for the ones who first spoke them or wrote them down and what they meant to those who heard them or read them.* That is when the historical or cultural setting becomes important. Because the Bible was written in various time periods, we must understand its historical context. How a given truth applies to us must be understood through the attitudes, settings, lifestyle, and political structure of the times in which it was given. We begin to understand the Bible when we learn what was said, who said it, how it was said, where it was said, when it was said, and why it was said.

In this first step we need to remember that nothing spoken or written in Scripture was spoken or written to us living in the twenty-first century. Moses and the prophets were speaking to the children of Israel. Jesus was speaking to his disciples, the crowds, and various individuals. When the apostles wrote the Gospels and when Paul, Peter, James, and others wrote the other books of the New Testament, they were writing them for certain hearers or readers of their time. It's unlikely that any of the authors of Scripture understood that some 2000 to 3000 years later their writings would exist as the authoritative holy Bible for all the world to read.

The point is, they wrote what they wrote within a historical context, to an audience considerably different than us today. But even though the words of Scripture may not have been written specifically *to* us in the twenty-first century, that doesn't mean they weren't written *for* us as well as for the original recipients. So because God was revealing himself and his truth to a specific audience within a specific time in history, our first task is to interpret what he intended to communicate to them at the time.

THE RELEVANT TRUTH

But then comes the second very important step: *understanding what universal, relevant truth God is revealing to us right now.* Remember that the Bible is no ordinary literary work. It is the living Word coming from the living God. And his Word is relevant to each person living today and applicable to each and every situation in life, no matter what the cultural setting. The writer of the book of Hebrews said,

> The word of God is full of living power. It is sharper than the sharpest knife, cutting deep into our innermost thoughts and desires. It exposes us for what we really are. Nothing in all creation can hide from him. Everything is naked and exposed before his eyes. This is the God to whom we must explain all that we have done (Hebrews 4:12-13 NLT).

The truth of God's Word transcends history, cultures, customs, languages, and time lines. So when we are trying to understand what God wanted the people to know when he gave them his Word, we are also wanting to understand what he wants us to know today in our own lives. We need to remember that the Scripture is an ever-living document made real by the Holy Spirit. We can "know these things," Paul wrote, "because God has revealed them to us by his Spirit, and the Spirit searches out everything and shows us even God's deep secrets" (1 Corinthians 2:10 NLT).

The apostle Paul goes on to say that he spoke with words given to him by the Spirit "using the Spirit's words to explain spiritual truths" (1 Corinthians 2:13). There are truths from the Old and New Testaments that the Holy Spirit wants to apply to us. Our response can then be, "God, what do you intend for me to experience from the words of your book? My heart is open. Help the truth of Scripture penetrate my innermost being." The Bible is real and relevant today in every culture because God, the author of the book, is real and relevant to all of his creation.*

---

* For more on how the Bible is relevant and how to experience it, read *How to Experience Your Bible*. See the back of this book for more information about *How to Experience Your Bible*.

59.

HOW IS IT THAT THE BIBLE GETS SO MISINTERPRETED?

The Bible is from God, and so you might think that when Christians read it they would all get the same message. But there are many different teachings coming out of the Bible because people misinterpret it. What is the main cause of this misinterpretation? How is it that even honest Christians who are seeking the truth can misinterpret the meaning of God's Word?

There are a number of reasons for this. And we all need to learn how to correctly interpret the Word.* But there are two crucial mistakes people often make when they try to interpret the meaning of the Bible:

- They take a Scripture verse or words out of context.
- They inject their own views or emotions into the text.

And when this happens we misinterpret the meaning and message of God's Word.

LACK OF CONTEXT

Imagine you walk by me (Sean) as I'm talking to three or four of my friends. You overhear me say, "No, I'm leaving Stephanie next week. Scottie will stay with her." You don't stop to inquire further but step over to one of your friends. The following is what you could say.

"Did you hear the latest about Sean and Stephanie McDowell?"

"No," your friend replies. "What?"

"I just overheard Sean say he's leaving her next week, and she's going to get custody of their boy."

Shocked, your friend glances over toward me. "I can't believe it. There's another one of those Christian speakers who's always emphasizing relationship and can't live up to his own message. It's really a shame!"

---

* See "How Do You Correctly Interpret the Bible?" on page 173.

What just happened? Did you accurately interpret my words? You would have heard me correctly because I did say I was leaving my wife next week and Scottie, our son, was staying with her. But what you didn't hear were the sentences before and after. Here are the words in context:

"I guess you're excited about the upcoming speaking tour in Canada," my friend says.

"Yeah, I'm really looking forward to it," I reply.

"You're leaving later this week, right? Is Scottie going with you?"

"No, I'm leaving Stephanie next week," I reply. "Scottie will stay with her." I pause. "I'll only be gone a week, so it won't be too hard on us. I really hate being away from the family."

The point is, we can miss the true meaning of what is said or written when we take words out of context. Proper interpretation requires proper context. We can keep Scripture within context when we understand the setting of a passage—what comes immediately before a verse and what comes after. Whether it's a statement like "I'm leaving Stephanie" or a Scripture passage that we isolate and fail to understand within the whole of the narrative, we are in danger of misinterpreting the meaning.[41]

PUTTING IN YOUR OWN VIEWS

The other main reason people misinterpret the Bible is that they inject their own views into a passage. Sometimes people are guilty of using Bible verses just to make their own point. And when you take verses out of context you can make just about any point you want to. But also, sometimes a person's past experience and unhealthy relationships with others keep them from making correct interpretations.

The things you have done or relationships you have had, especially with family members, play a critical role in shaping your view of yourself and your life. And that shaping often negatively affects how you personally approach and interpret the Bible—because how you related to your parents and they to you significantly influenced your perception of God. For example, if you grew up with authoritarian parents and felt their disapproval or felt distant from them, you will likely project those feelings onto your relationship with God. You will naturally bring that distorted lens to your reading of Scripture, causing you to see him as an authoritarian, disapproving figure.

For me (Josh), growing up in an alcoholic home heavily colored my view of God, the Scriptures, and the Christian life, and consequently I misinterpreted some passages of the Bible. You see, I developed a pattern of thinking and behavior that made me what psychologists call a "rescuer." Each time I saw my father try to hurt my mom, I would step in and try to prevent her from being hurt. This became a lifelong psychological and emotional pattern for me. I always tried to rescue hurting, struggling people.

When I became a Christian I continued this unhealthy behavioral pattern, though I didn't realize it was unhealthy. Each time I saw someone hurting, my compulsion kicked in. But I didn't know it was a compulsion; I thought it was compassion. I thought I was exhibiting godlike love. When I read the passage "Bear one another's burdens, and thereby fulfill the law of Christ" (Galatians 6:2 NASB), I thought it meant I was emotionally responsible to solve the person's problem by removing whatever burden they had. I thought I was fulfilling the "law of Christ" and acting as he would. In reality, I was doing myself harm and, in most cases, doing the person a disservice. All this was reinforced in my life because I was misinterpreting God's Word by viewing it through my dysfunctional "rescuing" lenses.

It took the help of others so I could see this passage clearly. I learned that Scripture didn't teach that bearing another person's burden meant taking responsibility for that person's problem or hurt. Rather, it means coming alongside and gently helping a person lift the weight. Bearing the burdens of others doesn't mean *taking responsibility for their problem*; it means *being responsible to them*—to comfort, encourage, and support them in their pain or difficulties.

Yes, Galatians 6:2 tells us that we are to "bear one another's burdens." The key to my turnaround was the passage I discovered just three more verses down the page. Galatians 6:5 declares, "Each one will bear his own load" (NASB).

Now, this may sound confusing at first, but it comes together when you realize that there is an important difference between a "burden" and a "load." The Greek word for *burden* is *baros,* which denotes a heavy weight. Jesus used this word when describing the workers toiling in the vineyard who have "borne the burden (*baros*) and the scorching heat of the day" (Matthew 20:12 NASB). This was a heavy burden to bear.

We all face situations that bear down heavily on us, and God is pleased that others experience Galatians 6:2 with us by coming alongside to support us in our difficulty. Consider the image of a man carrying a heavy beam across his shoulders. Now watch as two friends come alongside him. They put their shoulders on either side of the beam and help him lift his load. That is the picture here. When we are burdened down with things like an injury, an illness, the loss of a job, or loss of a loved one, we need support; we need others to help us lift our heavy load.

In verse 5 Paul uses a different word for *burden* or *weight*. He says, "Each one shall bear his own load" (Galatians 6:5 NASB). This is the Greek word *phortion*, which refers to something with little weight that is carried, like a supply pack a first-century soldier would carry into the field. A more natural term is given in the New Living Translation: "We are each responsible for our own conduct" (Galatians 6:5). In other words, this load is your assignment, and bearing it is your responsibility alone. It's the same idea Paul was conveying when he said, "Each of us will give a personal account to God" (Romans 14:12).

We all have personal responsibilities, and when we fail in our responsibilities—by using poor judgment or making wrong choices or harboring bad attitudes—we must face up to the consequences. To step in and remove the natural and corrective consequences of people's irresponsible behavior may rob them of valuable lessons—lessons that may be crucial to their continued growth and maturity.[42]

We misinterpret the Bible when we take words or even verses out of context and when we inject our own views or dysfunctional emotions into the text. There is a correct means of interpreting God's Word, which requires careful study and following a specific process. We will discuss that in the next question: "How Do You Correctly Interpret the Bible?"

60.

HOW DO YOU CORRECTLY
INTERPRET THE BIBLE?

The Bible teaches many truths and doctrines. When God inspired his prophets and apostles he no doubt wanted us to understand *his* one clear intended meaning. The apostle Peter said that "no prophecy of Scripture is a matter of one's own interpretation" (2 Peter 1:20 NASB). So we all need to seek the objective meaning—God's interpretation—of each doctrine or truth of Scripture. That is why Paul challenged us to "be diligent...accurately handling the word of truth" (2 Timothy 2:15 NASB). Our task as Christians is to interpret the words of Scripture to understand their intended meaning. So how do we correctly interpret the Bible in order to know what God intended us to know?

To interpret the teachings of Scripture correctly and truly requires that we draw out God's meaning. We are not to create the meaning ourselves or read into a text what *we* think it is teaching. When people put their particular slant on a passage or inject their own ideas, it is not hard to see how we can end up having different and contradictory views on a particular truth.* But much of this can be avoided if we follow a process to discover God's meaning of a truth. This process is called *exegesis*.

Exegesis is from the Greek word *exegeomai*, which means "to make known, to unfold in teaching, to declare by making known." The word is used by John when he says that Jesus "has *revealed* God to us" (John 1:18). The New American Standard Bible translated this phrase as, "He has *explained* him."

To properly interpret, or explain and reveal, the meaning of a passage of Scripture we must engage in this process of exegesis. We do this by asking various questions about the passage to determine answers to *what, where, why, how,* and so on. And in the process we do the following:

---

* See "How Is It that the Bible Gets So Misinterpreted?" on page 169.

173

1. examine the text to understand its grammatical construct;

2. understand the meaning of individual words—literally, figuratively, culturally, and so on;

3. discover the historical context, such as the author, cultural setting, time frame, and so on;

4. examine the message within the context of paragraphs, chapters, individual books, and the entire scope of scriptural truth; and

5. understand that the timeless truth applied to those it was first written to and then understand how that timeless truth applies to us today.*

To accurately interpret Scripture involves a number of carefully employed tools and disciplines.† For now let's briefly note two key elements of biblical interpretation: understanding the meaning of words and understanding the context of those words.

THE MEANING OF WORDS

Language is composed of words, which are the building blocks of ideas. And when we assemble words together in paragraphs they become the basic unit of communication. This is true of any literary work. And the Bible is a literary work of words and paragraphs that communicate God's truth to us. But how we interpret those words is important, because words change their meaning as they are associated with other words and phrases. So are the words of the Bible to be interpreted literally, figuratively, or what? And this is where understanding the use of metaphors and grammar comes in.

Metaphor. Part of interpretation is applying common sense, rather than always taking words literally. We can understand passages better if we allow language to speak in ordinary ways, instead of imposing some kind of special, artificial standard for language usage in the Bible. For example, when Jesus said, "I am the bread of life" in John 6:35, did he mean he was a loaf of ground grain mixed with yeast and baked? No—we know he

---

* See "How Can Teachings from the Ancient Cultures of the Bible Be Relevant to Us Today?" on page 166.

† To learn more on how to better interpret the Bible see *Experience Your Bible*, described in the back of this book.

was metaphorically saying he provides sustenance for our spiritual life just as bread provides sustenance for our physical life. But if we try to make biblical metaphors read literally we will misinterpret their true meaning. As we said earlier, the Bible is literature, and the same linguistic principles apply to it as to other writings. While it is correct to believe the Bible is true, we must allow metaphors, similes, and analogies to be what they are, and not force them to be literal.

Grammar. In interpreting a passage we must not only look for metaphors, but also give attention to grammar. Grammar involves such things as verb tenses, questions, commands, subjects, and objects. These elements determine the structure of the language, and they are important factors in determining exactly what is being said. Understanding the root meaning of the words in Scripture and their grammatical usage helps us interpret the truth God wants us to understand.

THE MEANING OF THE WORDS WITHIN CONTEXT

So many erroneous and contradictory teachings among churches and Christians arise by taking Scripture out of context. And when this is done we miss the true meaning of what God is saying to us.

Literary context. Context is important to exegete a passage. This is often done by understanding the setting of a passage—what comes immediately before and what comes after. Remember when I (Josh) stated in the previous question that I struggled with understanding Galatians 6:2? It wasn't that I misread "Bear one another's burdens," it was that I was not seeing it within context. When I read three verses down and examined the Greek words for "burden" and "load" I was able to understand verse 2 within the context of the whole passage.

So when we read a passage out of context we are in danger of reading another meaning into the text that simply isn't there. Scholars call this *eisegesis* or "reading into." Most errors of interpretation come from reading into Scripture a meaning that just isn't there. And much of that can be avoided by reading the text within context.

But we need to see more than a few verses before and after a biblical truth to interpret it within context. We need to see it within the context of the chapter and in fact the entire Bible. And that is where cross-referencing comes in.

Cross-referencing simply means the process of following a topic or a word from one verse to another within the Bible to discover all it has to say on the subject. The power of cross-referencing is in its authority. Since we are allowing Scripture to interpret Scripture, we can depend on the correctness of our findings.

Several resources are available to help us locate cross-references. Study Bibles on the market have cross-references listed in a separate column beside the verse. Your Bible may also have a concordance. Another useful tool is a chain-reference Bible. The original chain-reference Bible, still available today, is the *Thompson Chain Reference Bible*. A chain reference has elaborate marginal references and an elaborate reference index, which help you trace a given topic throughout the entire Bible.*

Historical context. The Bible was written in various historical time periods. The attitudes, setting, lifestyle, and political structure of a certain time will affect the understanding of a passage. Therefore, in order to exegete a Bible passage we must see it within its historical and cultural context. As we stated before, the Scripture may not have been specifically written *to* us in the twenty-first century, but that doesn't mean it wasn't written *for* us—it was. But to understand what God is saying to us today we must understand it within its cultural context and then properly apply his truth to our own culture and personal lives.

When we read the Bible we are entering into the past. The Scriptures were written over a 1500-year span. Within that time frame significant cultural, political, and sociological changes took place. As we understand the meaning of the words and discover the literary and historical context, we are in a position to better understand what God is saying to us. And as we do, the meaning of his Word can be revealed and applied to our lives.

---

* See "What Are the Resources I Need to Accurately Interpret the Bible?" on page 223.

61.

CAN CHRISTIANS HOLD CONTRADICTORY TEACHINGS FROM THE BIBLE AND STILL BE IN UNITY?

There are hundreds of different denominations within Christianity, all of which claim to be Christian and doctrinally correct. Yet there is a wide variance in what they believe and teach. Many of these churches don't cooperate and work together because of their differences. Is this the right way to be? Can't Christians hold to different and contradictory teaching of the Bible and still be in unity? Or must there always be differences among Christians and churches?

UNITY IN LOVE

Jesus told his disciples to love each other. In fact, he said, "Your love for one another will prove to the world that you are my disciples" (John 13:35). The mark of a true follower of Christ is the love he or she has for others, especially the devotion shown toward other brothers and sisters in Christ. Jesus prayed about his followers to his heavenly Father this way: "I pray that they will all be one, just as you and I are one" (John 17:21). The apostle Paul talked about the unity of God's people: "There is one body and one Spirit, just as you have been called to one glorious hope for the future. There is one Lord, one faith, one baptism, and one God and Father, who is over all and in all and living through all" (Ephesians 4:4-5).

It sounds like God's plan is to have all Christians who are truly following Christ and the Bible to live in unity with one another. So what is the problem?

It is true that some Christians condemn others for not believing as they do. But far more of them simply have different views on certain biblical teachings and do not allow it to disrupt their unity with each other.

I (Sean) am in unity with my wife, Stephanie. But we have a different taste in cars; a different preference in literature; my favorite food is different than hers; I prefer action movies, she likes romance; the list could go on and on. We see things differently and come at life from different angles. But this diversity doesn't divide us—rather, it makes us stronger as a couple. And when we do disagree, we agree to disagree. Stephanie's strength is often my weakness, and her weakness is often my strength. We complement one another this way, and it makes our unity even more unified.

Just because Christians see things differently in Scripture doesn't mean they need to be at odds with one another. And many Christian groups and churches we work with do relate to those who differ with them in the spirit of Christian liberty. Most Christians who have adopted a Calvinistic theology love those who are Wesleyan-Arminian. Wesleyan-Arminians love Calvinists. Premillennialists love postmillennialists. Baptists love Nazarenes, and Lutherans love those within the Assemblies of God. Not all relate with others in Christian liberty but many, many do. Even after long and honest study of Scripture, there are areas that are open to different interpretation, and we all need to be careful not to be dogmatic in these areas of difference.

THE ESSENTIALS

However, there are certain biblical teachings that are so important and foundational that they require clear agreement. The apostles warned that false teaching would crop up (2 Corinthians 11:13-14). And they laid down certain essentials of the Christian faith that all followers of Christ needed to embrace in order to stay true to him. One was about the person of Jesus. "If someone claims to be a prophet," John said, "and does not acknowledge the truth about Jesus, that person is not from God" (1 John 4:3). The apostles made it clear that it was necessary to believe that Jesus was God in human form and that he died that we might be brought into relationship with God. That became a condition of Christian unity in the early church.*

The apostle Paul laid down another essential of the faith when he said,

> If Christ has not been raised, then your faith is useless and you are still guilty of your sins. In that case, all who have died believing in Christ are lost!...But in fact, Christ has been raised from the dead (1 Corinthians 15:17-18,20).

The bodily resurrection of Jesus was an essential belief to early Christianity. Jesus said,

---

* See "Did Jesus Really Claim to Be God?" on page 109.

I am the resurrection and the life. Those who believe in me, even though they die like everyone else, will live again. They are given eternal life for believing in me and will never perish (John 11:25-26 NLT).*

So there are certain essentials that must be agreed upon. Other essentials include belief in original sin, Christ's atonement for sin, and justification through faith.†

———————

As Christians we need to be in unity with fellow believers even though we may differ on various biblical teachings that are not completely clear. These are nonessentials to the core truths of the faith. In these situations we are to give liberty to our brothers and sisters in Christ. But on the essentials, we must agree and, as Jude wrote, "defend the faith that God has entrusted once for all time to his holy people" (Jude 3).

And in that light, when agreement on the essentials cannot be found with those who claim to be Christ-followers, it is appropriate to break fellowship. This should not be done lightly or in a reactionary spirit. Rather, it should be done prayerfully and in a loving and Christlike spirit. It is important to be within a church and among Christ-followers who teach and adhere to the essentials of the faith. And when you do, you become a living representative of Christ's love to the world around you.

Paul wrote to the church in Philippi,

Is there any encouragement from belonging to Christ? Any comfort from his love? Any fellowship together in the Spirit? Are your hearts tender and compassionate? Then make me truly happy by agreeing wholeheartedly with each other, loving one another, and working together with one mind and purpose (Philippians 2:1-2).

———————

* See "Why Is Jesus' Resurrection So Central to Christianity?" on page 130.

† For a full treatment of the 12 foundational truths of Christianity see *The Unshakable Truth: How You Can Experience the 12 Essentials of a Relevant Faith*. See the back of this book for more information about *The Unshakable Truth*.

62.

ARE ALL THE OLD TESTAMENT
LAWS BINDING ON US TODAY?

The Old Testament was written to the children of Israel (the Jewish people). So some people say that most of it doesn't apply to Christians today. And so while we may get some good stories from the Old Testament, is it really binding on Christians?

First, it is important to realize that neither the Old nor the New Testament was written to people living in the twenty-first century. The Old Testament audience was the children of Israel, and the New Testament was written to a Jewish and Gentile audience in the first century.* But that doesn't mean the truth of Scripture isn't relevant to or binding on us today.

The Bible was written within certain historical contexts, all quite different from ours today. But even though the words of Scripture may not have been written specifically *to* us, that doesn't mean they weren't written *for* us. Scripture is God's universal and relevant truth that is applicable to all people, in all places, for all times. Both the Old and the New Testament messages transcend history, cultures, customs, languages, and time lines. So to interpret what God is saying to us in the twenty-first century we must first identify the universal truths of Scripture that were applied in ancient times in order to understand how they apply to us today.†

With that said, the Old Testament is rich with truth that is applicable to us today. However, as we stated above, we must understand its historical context in order to understand its meaning to us. God made a promise to Abraham—a covenant—that included his raising up a nation, and through Abraham's descendants he would send a Savior, the Redeemer of the world. And the Old Testament is the story of God's faithful and loving relationship with his people, the children of Israel. And so it is understandable that certain promises, conditions, and instructions to Israel would not apply to everyone.

---

* See "How Can Teachings from the Ancient Cultures of the Bible Be Relevant to Us Today?" on page 166.

† See " Can Christians Hold Contradictory Teachings from the Bible and Still Be in Unity?" on page 177.

THE OLD TESTAMENT IN CONTEXT OF THE NEW

But to understand how the truth of the Old Testament applies universally and to Christians today we must interpret it within the context of the New Testament. The apostle Paul said,

> Why then, was the law given? It was given alongside the promise to show people their sin. But the law was designed to last only until the coming of the child who was promised [Jesus]… The law was our guardian until Christ came; it protected us until we could be made right with God through faith. And now that the way of faith has come, we no longer need the law as our guardian (Galatians 3:19,24-25).

What Paul was saying is that the law was our guardian or tutor. It was like a teacher guiding and instructing a child until the student had come of age. The law fulfilled its purpose by guiding God's people to the one who would write his laws and ways on their hearts. God didn't want people focusing on all the laws and rules in the first place. He wanted them to focus on him in a relationship. Following his ways would then be a natural by-product of that relationship. And all that came into perfect view when Jesus showed up on the stage of human history.

Jesus made it clear that *he* was the context for interpreting the Old Testament. He said, "Don't misunderstand why I have come. I did not come to abolish the law of Moses or the writings of the prophets. No, I came to accomplish their purpose" (Matthew 5:17). He actually fulfilled the ceremonial laws of Moses and satisfied God's justice in dealing with our sin.

The ceremonial laws that God had given the children of Israel dealt with animal sacrifices, a priesthood, a temple, and numerous festivals to observe. These laws were a means or system to deal with sin, and to satisfy God's holy and just nature. He wanted his people to enjoy a relationship with him. The sacrificial system of the Old Testament was the means of receiving forgiveness and obtaining a relationship with him for the children of Israel. But that system and his forgiveness was actually based on the future coming of Christ, who would be the perfect sacrifice.

The reason we no longer need to follow the Old Testament ceremonial laws is that God's Son became our perfect sacrificial Lamb for all time (see Hebrews 3–10). That is what Jesus meant when he said he fulfilled the law.

The law required a substitute, a perfect sacrifice to gain our redemption. Simply being obedient to a set of rules and following a system of sacrificing animals was not the solution. Faith in the perfect sacrifice of Jesus was the solution, and of course Christ provided that. So now following the ceremonial laws given to Israel is not needed or necessary. Accepting Christ as our sacrifice is what is needed—and that is what is necessary.

The civil laws. The same can be said about what is known as Israel's civil laws. Throughout the first five books of the Old Testament the children of Israel were not only given the Ten Commandments (the moral law), but specifics on how God's law was to be enforced within their nation. There were very specific things that God commanded his people to do, as well as how to do them, when to do them, and the consequences and remedies for disobedience. While those laws were specifically for Israel and were not intended to translate to our modern civil laws, it doesn't mean we are not to learn from them. We can certainly see that God desires a system of justice. He wants us as followers of him to come to the defense of the weak or to those who are mistreated (see the book of James). Civil laws are needed and necessary for a civil society to operate.

The moral law. And certainly the *moral law* of the Old Testament, often referred to as the Ten Commandments, reflects God's universal truth to all of us. Each of the Ten Commandments is repeated in the New Testament, except observance of the Sabbath day. And that one is in effect repeated in the truth that as Christ's body, the church, we are to love each other and worship together. The writer of the book of Hebrews said, "Let us not neglect our meeting together, as some people do, but encourage one another" (Hebrews 10:25). So certainly the moral law of the Old Testament is binding on and applicable to us today.

———————

When we read the Old Testament we must understand God's truth within the historical context of the children of Israel. And when we do, it becomes clear how God wants his eternal truth to be applied in our personal lives and the life of the twenty-first-century world.

63.

ARE ANY OF THE JEWISH FESTIVALS IN THE BIBLE MEANINGFUL TO CHRISTIANS TODAY?

The Old Testament often mentioned festivals that the children of Israel were to observe. We know that the Jewish ceremonial law with its sacrificial system has been fulfilled in Jesus. So we are not required as Christians to observe those many Jewish festivals. But are any of these festivals meaningful to Christians today? Do they have significance to any New Testament teachings or to the Christian life?

Yes—a number, if not all, of the Jewish festivals can be meaningful to us today. Many Christians, for example, find rich meaning in three of the Jewish festivals: the observances of Passover, Pentecost, and the Feast of Shelters.

In Exodus, God commanded every one of the children of Israel to "celebrate three festivals in my honor" (Exodus 23:14). The first was the Festival of Unleavened Bread, or Passover. For centuries Jewish families have gathered at sundown of the fourteenth day of the first month of the Hebrew calendar to celebrate this festival.

THE FEAST OF PASSOVER

The meal of Passover (*pesach*) includes a roast lamb, bitter salad greens, and bread made without yeast. During the meal the father, with the assistance of the children, retells the story of God redeeming Israel from Egyptian bondage. They explain how the death angel came over the land to kill the firstborn male of each family. But God had told his people they would be spared if they observed the Passover as he instructed. Each Israelite family was to choose a lamb or a young goat, kill it, and smear its blood on the top and sides of the door frame of their houses. In the evening they were to eat roast lamb with bitter herbs and bread made without yeast. That night at midnight God's death angel killed all the firstborn sons within Egypt. But those with the sacrificial blood placed on their houses were passed over (Exodus 12).

From that day forward Jewish families have been celebrating their redemption out of Egyptian slavery, because the death of Egypt's firstborn was the final blow that caused Pharaoh to free Israel from slavery.

But what is so significant to Christians is what happened some 1400 years after the first Passover. In Jerusalem a group of Jewish men gathered to observe this special festival. But something very strange took place. The man leading the Passover took the unleavened bread, passed it around to those in the room, and said the most extraordinary thing: "Take this and eat it, for this is my body" (Matthew 26:26). He then took a cup of wine and passed it around in customary Passover fashion, but again said the strangest of things: "Each of you drink from it," he instructed, "for this is my blood, which confirms the covenant between God and his people. It is poured out as a sacrifice to forgive the sins of many" (Matthew 26:27-28). This Jewish man was re-interpreting the entire Passover celebration. He was claiming to *be* the bread; he was claiming that the wine was *his* blood. This had to baffle those in attendance.

This man had told his followers before that he was "the bread of life" (John 6:35). This was the same man that the prophet John the Baptist made a bold declaration about when he saw him coming toward him. "Look!" John said, "The Lamb of God who takes away the sin of the world!" (John 1:29). Within hours of this momentous Passover celebration, the man called Jesus would be led away, brutally beaten, and cruelly nailed to a cross to bleed and die. Just over 1400 years after the very first redemption celebration by God's people, this Jesus of Nazareth, God's firstborn, celebrated himself being the Passover Lamb to be offered as redemption to a human race in bondage to sin. What a feast for Christians to celebrate!

The Passover is not just a Jewish celebration. It is a celebration for all those who have been redeemed by the atoning sacrifice of Jesus Christ.

> You know that God paid a ransom to save you from the empty
> life you inherited from your ancestors. And the ransom he

paid was not mere gold or silver. It was the precious blood of Christ, the sinless, spotless Lamb of God (1 Peter 1:18-19).

And so lambs and bulls and goats no longer need to be sacrificed because "now, once for all time, he [Jesus] has appeared at the end of the age to remove sin by his own death as a sacrifice" (Hebrews 9:26). The Passover is a celebration all Christians can celebrate because of God's redemptive plan through Christ.

THE FESTIVAL OF PENTECOST

Fifty days from the beginning of Passover, Jewish families were commanded to give an offering to God from the first of their crops. They were to "count off seven full weeks. Keep counting until the day after the seventh Sabbath, fifty days later" (Leviticus 23:15-16). This time was called the Festival of *Shavuot*. But for centuries, in addition to celebrating their harvest, Jewish families have also celebrated the revelation of God through his written Word given to Moses on Mount Sinai. So along with making a crop offering, Jewish families would gather and praise God for revealing himself as dramatically as he did on the day he showed himself to Moses and gave the commandments "written by the finger of God" (Exodus 31:18).

Now fast-forward to the first century. Imagine Jesus' disciples thrilled and almost beside themselves at Jesus' resurrection. The Passover Lamb of God had been sacrificed and Jewish redemption was a reality. Their Messiah was back and they asked, "Lord, has the time come for you to free Israel and restore our kingdom?" (Acts 1:6). It was only ten days before the festival of Shavuot (*Pentecost* in the Greek), and what a perfect time for the Son of God to reveal himself as the powerful God of the heavenly kingdom. Pentecost celebrated God's revelation at Sinai, why not the Son of God's revelation at Jerusalem—truly a new kingdom celebration.

But to the disciples' amazement, Jesus ascends to heaven. Yet just before that, he told them to go back to the city and wait for the promise of the Father (see Luke 24:49). Perhaps confused and maybe even frustrated they followed Jesus' instructions. And ten days later 120 followers of Jesus gathered together in an upper room to celebrate Shavuot/Pentecost. Typically it would be with readings and prayers and thanking God for his powerful revelation at Mount Sinai. Yet on this particular Pentecost something extraordinary took place.

As the disciples were gathered, the Holy Spirit was revealed like a windstorm and "what looked like flames or tongues of fire appeared and settled on each of them" (Acts 2:3). This festival changed from a celebration of God revealing himself through his Holy Word to God also revealing himself through his Holy Spirit. And instead of offering up their first harvest, the disciples *were* the first harvest—the first church!

Pentecost is not just a Jewish celebration. It is a celebration of God's gift of his Holy Spirit to every Christian. We can thank God for giving us his Word and his Spirit, who enters our lives to make us his child:

> You received God's Spirit when he adopted you as his own children. Now we call him, "Abba, Father." For his Spirit joins with our spirit to affirm that we are God's children. And since we are his children, we are his heirs. In fact, together with Christ we are heirs of God's glory (Romans 8:15-17).

THE FESTIVAL OF SHELTERS

The last of these three festivals is the *Festival of Shelters* (*Sukkot),* or the *Festival of Ingathering.* God commanded the children of Israel to live in makeshift shelters for seven days every year. "This will remind each new generation of Israelites that their ancestors had to live in shelters when I rescued them from the land of Egypt. I, the Lord, am your God" (Leviticus 23:43 nlt).

For centuries, during the fall of the year, Jewish families have celebrated *Sukkot* (Hebrew, meaning "booth" or "hut"). For seven days they are to eat in their huts and "celebrate with joy before the Lord your God" (Leviticus 23:40). As the final festival, it marks the completion of both the harvest season and the festival cycle. It therefore serves as a special time of celebrating the fullness of God's creative and redemptive work and, furthermore, the *rest* of God. It is to be a time to remember and reflect upon all God has done and give him glory. Yet the key significance of this festival is that it serves as a rehearsal and celebration of the future glory of God for Israel.

God gave the prophet Zechariah a vision of the coming Messiah, the restoration of Israel, and the restoration of all things. The prophet saw a time when "the Lord will be king over all the earth. On that day there will be one Lord—his name alone will be worshipped" (Zechariah 14:9). The apostle Paul spoke of a time in human history "that at the name of Jesus [the Messiah] every knee should bow, in heaven and on earth and under the earth, and every tongue confess that Jesus Christ is Lord, to the glory of God the Father" (Philippians 2:10-11).

It is in this restoration context that Zechariah declares that "the survivors from all the nations that have attacked Jerusalem will go up year after year to worship the King, the LORD Almighty, and to celebrate the Festival of Tabernacles [*Sukkot*]" (Zechariah 14:16 NIV). God had told his people to "be joyful at your festival...for the LORD your God will bless you in all your harvest and in all the work of your hands, and your joy will be complete" (Deuteronomy 16:14-15 NIV). But what Zechariah was no doubt pointing to was the ultimate joy made complete when all things would be restored to God's original design and "the tabernacle of God is among men, and He will dwell among them" (Revelation 21:3 NASB).

God has made a promise to Israel that they will have a permanent home and that their Messiah will reign forever. But that is far more than a Jewish celebration. Every child of God who has accepted Jesus as Savior and future Messiah can celebrate the promise of his second coming, when all the redeemed can say,

> Look, God's home is now among his people! He will live with them, and they will be his people. God himself will be with them. He will wipe every tear from their eyes, and there will be no more death or sorrow or crying or pain (Revelation 21:3-4).

This is a unique festival for Christians because this celebration is the only one out of the three at which God has not shown up—at least not yet. God the Son literally came in human flesh to celebrate Passover and literally became the Passover Lamb. God the Spirit literally came to celebrate Pentecost so he could literally live in us. But God has yet to literally show up to celebrate *Sukkot* with us. He will no doubt do that at his second coming, the time Jesus referred to in his Passover meal some 2000 years ago, when he said, "Mark my words—I will not drink wine again until the day I drink it new with you in my Father's kingdom" (Matthew 26:29). *Sukkot*, the Festival of Shelters, is certainly a time Christians can celebrate the anticipated second coming of Christ.

All three of these celebrations are excellent times to teach and reinforce the basics of the Christian faith with your church or your own family.

Because there has been such renewed interest in these three Jewish festivals we have recreated them as mealtime Judeo-Christian celebrations for Christian families and churches. The Passover is our "Redemption Celebration," Pentecost is our "Revelation Celebration," and the Festival of Shelters is our "Restoration Celebration." You can find these, along with all the details and handouts to perform them, in our book *The Unshakable Truth*. Simply go online to **Josh.org/celebrations** and download them for free. Take advantage of these to instill within your family a heart of gratitude for what God has done and a hopeful expectation of what he is going to do.

64.

WHAT IS THE REAL PURPOSE
OF THE BIBLE?

S ome people say the Bible is a handbook of the Christian religion, and its purpose is to lay out a set of rules and teachings that establish Christianity. Others claim the Bible tells us how to get to heaven and provides a roadmap for how to get there. Why did God give us his Book? What story does it tell? And what does that story have to do with us? Scripture itself gives us those answers.

A DOCTRINAL PURPOSE

One of the reasons God gave us the Scriptures is to inform us as to what we should believe. These beliefs become our authority for determining correct doctrine. This is to say there is a *doctrinal purpose for God's Word.* It gives us rational truths we can understand with our minds. These truths are doctrinal beliefs that make up Christian theology.

Many people shy away from the idea of theology. Yet theology is actually the study of God. So in a sense we are all "theologians." We all have ideas about who God is and what he is like, yet we rarely think of that as knowing "theology." But one of the clear purposes of Scripture is unabashedly theological—to reveal God for who he is. He wants us to know what he is like, how his ways differ from ours, and how he sees life in contrast to how we see it.

Doctrine does matter. By understanding what the Scriptures reveal about God, for example, we actually understand what he reveals about us. When we see all of life through his eyes we gain what is called a *biblical worldview*—a correct view about reality that tells us how the world came to be, who we are as human beings, how to know right from wrong, and so on. The doctrinal truths of Scripture act as boundaries that keep us aligned with correct beliefs so we can see life as God wants us to see it.

A BEHAVIORAL PURPOSE

The Bible also teaches us how to live. It is full of instructions, laws, and commands of what to do and what not to do. That is why we can say there is a *behavioral purpose for God's Word*. When the Bible says, "Follow this way," "avoid those places," "abstain from those actions," or "embrace those thoughts," it is instructing us how to live rightly.

Have you ever wondered why doing right most often produces good results and wrong living often results in negative consequences? Generally that's because 1) doctrinal truths of the Bible provide a correct view of God and his ways; and 2) when we embrace his thinking and live accordingly, we reap the benefits of godliness.

On the other hand, harboring incorrect beliefs about God and his ways distorts our values, making it unlikely that our actions will be right. The natural fallout will most likely be that we suffer the consequences of wrong living. "The LORD grants wisdom! From his mouth come knowledge and understanding. He grants a treasure of good sense to the godly. He is their shield, protecting those who walk with integrity" (Proverbs 2:7-8). So another reason God gave us his Word is so we can live out his truth correctly. The doctrines and commands of Scripture then act as two guardrails that guide us down a path of righteousness.

A RELATIONAL PURPOSE

There are a lot of commands found in the Bible. But there is one that is called the Great Commandment. Jesus said it like this:

> "You must love the Lord your God with all your heart, all your soul, and all your mind." This is the first and greatest commandment. A second is equally important: "Love your neighbor as yourself" (Matthew 22:37-39).

What Jesus was doing here was making a vital connection between truth (biblical beliefs and instruction) and relationships. This was something the religious leaders of Jesus' day failed to understand and do.

Of course, the Hebrew Scriptures are filled with the connection between truth and relationships, but sometimes we miss them. King David said in one of his psalms, "I am always aware of your unfailing love, and I have lived according to your truth" (Psalm 26:3). Then he prayed, "Teach me your ways, O LORD, that I may live according to your truth!" (Psalm 86:11). The Old Testament writers understood truth within the context of relationships. Jesus' declaration of the Great Commandment was simply a reframing of doctrinal beliefs and obedience and restoring them to their rightful place within the context of relationship, which had been lost by the religionists of his day. He was proclaiming that there was a *relational purpose for God's Word.* Jesus was telling us that right thinking and right living is to be placed within the context of right relationship. And if we fail to do this it will severely distort our thinking and our living.

God's ultimate intention from creation forward was for every person to enjoy the perfect circle of loving relationship that he enjoys within the Godhead. He wanted to disclose himself to humans so they could know him for who he is. This is the ultimate *doctrinal truth* that he intended for humans and the universe. He also wanted his creation to live within the boundaries of his ways, which was the only way they could enjoy all the goodness of a perfect world. This is the ultimate *behavioral truth* that he intended for us. God's intent was that the first couple, Adam and Eve, would believe that he was perfectly good and that when he gave them a command, he had their best interest at heart. His intent was that they would understand that he wanted them to love him dearly, and that his one command was given within the context of this *relational truth.* But they did not. And unfortunately, humans have been missing the relational context of God's truth ever since.

We may study God's Word for correct beliefs. We may even obey it for right behavior. But we must not forget why. The God of the Bible wants us to relationally experience his love and the love of those around us. We can then say this: *God gave us the Bible because he wants an intimate loving relationship with us, wants us to enjoy intimate loving relationships with one another, and wants our relationships together to extend us and his kingdom into eternity.*

65.

IS THE OLD TESTAMENT
HISTORICALLY RELIABLE?

The writing of the Old Testament began about 3400 years ago. Of course, none of the original manuscripts God inspired authors to write—called *autographa*—are in existence today. What we read now are printed copies translated from ancient handwritten copies of yet other copies of the original. This is because the Bible was composed and transmitted in an era before printing presses. All manuscripts had to be written by hand. Over time, the ink would fade, and the material the manuscript was written on would deteriorate. So if a document was to be preserved and passed down to the next generation, new copies had to be made, else the document would be lost forever. Of course, these copies were made just like the originals—by hand with fading ink on deteriorating materials.

But, you may rightly wonder, doesn't the making of hand-copied reproductions open up the whole transmission process to error? How do we know that a weary copier, blurry-eyed from lack of sleep, didn't skip a few critical words, or leave out whole sections of Genesis, or misquote some key verses in Isaiah? Bible critics say that the Bible is a collection of outdated writings that are riddled with inaccuracies and distortions.* So, how can we be sure that the Bibles available to us today reflect an accurate transmission of the originals?

God has not left us to wonder. He has miraculously supervised the transmission of the Scriptures to ensure they were relayed accurately from one generation to another.

THE WORK OF SCRIBES

One of the ways God ensured that the Old Testament would be relayed accurately was by choosing, calling, and cultivating a nation of men and

---

* See "Isn't the Bible Full of Errors and Contradictions?" on page 154.

women who took the Book of the Law very seriously. God commanded and instilled in the Jewish people a great reverence for the Scriptures. That attitude became such a part of the Jewish identity that a class of Jewish scholars called the *Sopherim*, from a Hebrew word meaning "scribes," arose between the fifth and third centuries BC. These custodians of the Hebrew Scriptures dedicated themselves to carefully preserving the ancient manuscripts and producing new copies when necessary.

The Sopherim were eclipsed by the *Talmudic* scribes, who guarded, interpreted, and commented on the sacred texts from about AD 100 to 500. The Talmudic scribes were followed by the better-known *Masoretic* scribes (about AD 500 to 900).

The Talmudic scribes, for example, established detailed and stringent disciplines for copying a manuscript. Their rules were so rigorous that when a new copy was complete, they would give the reproduction equal authority to that of its parent because they were thoroughly convinced they had an exact duplicate.

This was the class of people who, in the providence of God, were chosen to preserve the Old Testament text for centuries. A scribe would begin his day of transcribing by ceremonially washing his entire body. He would then garb himself in full Jewish dress before sitting at his desk. As he wrote, if he came to the Hebrew name of God, he could not begin writing the name with a quill newly dipped in ink for fear it would smear the page. Once he began writing that name, he could not stop or allow himself to be distracted. Even if a king were to enter the room, the scribe was obligated to continue without interruption until he finished penning the holy name of the one true God.

The Talmudic guidelines for copying manuscripts also required the following:

- The scroll must be made of the skin of a ceremonially clean animal.
- Each skin must contain a specified number of columns, equal throughout the entire book.
- The length of each column must extend no less than 48 lines and no more than 60 lines.
- The column breadth must consist of exactly 30 letters.

- The space of a thread must appear between every consonant.

- The breadth of nine consonants had to be inserted between each section.

- A space of three lines had to appear between each book.

- The fifth book of Moses (Deuteronomy) had to conclude exactly with a full line.

- Nothing—not even the shortest word—could be copied from memory; everything had to be copied letter by letter.

- The scribe must count the number of times each letter of the alphabet occurred in each book and compare it to the original.[43]

THE TEXT CONFIRMED

Until the mid-twentieth century, however, we had no way of knowing just how amazing the preservation of the Old Testament had been. As we related in question 54, before 1947, the oldest complete Hebrew manuscript dated to AD 900. But with the discovery of 223 biblical manuscripts and many more partial manuscripts and fragments in caves on the west side of the Dead Sea, we now have Old Testament manuscripts that have been dated by paleographers to around 125 BC. These Dead Sea Scrolls, as they are called, are a thousand years older than any previously known manuscripts.

But here's the exciting part: Once the Dead Sea Scrolls were compared with modern versions, the modern Hebrew Bible proved to be identical, word for word, in more than 95 percent of the text. (The other 5 percent consisted mainly of spelling variations. For example, of the 166 words in Isaiah 53, only 17 letters were in question. Of those, 10 letters were a matter of spelling and 4 were stylistic changes; the remaining 3 letters comprised the word *light,* which was added in verse 11.)[44]

In other words, the greatest manuscript discovery of all time revealed that a thousand years of copying the Old Testament had produced only excruciatingly minor variations, none of which altered the clear meaning of the text or brought the manuscript's fundamental integrity into question.

Critics will still make their pronouncements in contradiction to the evidence. However, the overwhelming weight of evidence affirms that God has preserved his Word and accurately relayed it through the centuries—so that when you pick up an Old Testament today, you can be utterly confident that you are holding a well-preserved, fully reliable document.*

---

* For a more comprehensive treatment of the reliability of the Old Testament see *More Evidence That Demands a Verdict*, chapter 4.

66.

IS THE NEW TESTAMENT HISTORICALLY RELIABLE?

an you be sure the New Testament you read is what God inspired Matthew, Mark, John, Paul, or Peter to write down? Remember that it was written roughly 2000 years ago. We of course don't have the original handwritten manuscripts, so how can you be sure the ancient copies we have today haven't been tampered with or distorted by people adding their own ideas? In other words, how can we be sure that the New Testament we have today is a reliable reproduction of what God inspired his writers to write?

A MULTIPLICITY OF MANUSCRIPTS

There were expert Hebrew scribes who made copies of the Old Testament manuscripts.* But that is not the case with the New Testament. There are several reasons for this: 1) The official Jewish leadership did not endorse Christianity; 2) the letters and histories circulated by the New Testament writers were not then thought of as official Scripture; and 3) these documents were not written in the Hebrew language, but rather in forms of Greek and Aramaic. Thus, the same formal disciplines were not followed in the transmission of these writings from one generation to another. In the case of the New Testament, God did a new thing to ensure that his Word would be accurately preserved for us and our children.

Historians evaluate the textual reliability of ancient literature according to two standards: 1) the time interval between the original and the earliest copy; and 2) how many manuscript copies are available.

For example, virtually everything we know today about Julius Caesar's exploits in the Gallic Wars (58 to 51 BC) is derived from ten manuscript copies of Caesar's work *The Gallic Wars*. The earliest of these copies dates to a little less than a thousand years from the time the original was written. Our modern text of Livy's *History of Rome* relies on 1 partial manuscript

* See "Is the Old Testament Historically Reliable?" on page 192.

and 19 much later copies that are dated from 400 to 1000 years *after* the original writing (see chart below).[45]

Textual Reliability Standards Applied to Classical Literature

Author	Book	Date written	Earliest existing copies	Time gap	Number of copies
Homer	*Iliad*	800 BC	c. 400 BC	c. 400 years	643
Herodotus	*History*	480–425 BC	c. AD 900	c. 1350 years	8
Thucydides	*History*	460–400 BC	c. AD 900	c. 1300 years	8
Plato		400 BC	c. AD 900	c. 1300 years	7
Demosthenes		300 BC	c. AD 1100	c. 1400 years	200
Caesar	*Gallic Wars*	100–44 BC	c. AD 900	c. 1000 years	10
Livy	*History of Rome*	59 BC–AD 17	AD 300s AD 900s	c. 400 years c. 1000 years	1 partial 19
Tacitus	*Annals*	AD 100	c. AD 1100	c. 1000 years	20
Pliny Secundus	*Natural History*	AD 61–113	c. AD 850	c. 750 years	7

By comparison, the text of Homer's *Iliad* is much more reliable. It is supported by 643 manuscript copies in existence today, with a mere 400-year time gap between the date of composition and the earliest of these copies.

The textual evidence for Livy and Homer is considered more than adequate for historians to use in validating the originals, but this evidence pales in comparison to what God performed in the case of the New Testament text.

THE NEW TESTAMENT HAS NO EQUAL

Using this accepted standard for evaluating the textual reliability of ancient writings, the New Testament stands alone. It has no equal. No other book of the ancient world can even approach its textual reliability. (See chart of "Textual Reliability Standards Applied to the Bible.")[46]

Nearly 25,000 manuscripts or fragments of manuscripts of the New Testament repose in the libraries and universities of the world. The earliest of these discovered so far is a fragment of John's Gospel, located in the John Rylands Library of the University of Manchester, England; it has been dated to within 50 years of when the apostle John penned the original![47]

Textual Reliability Standards Applied to the Bible

Author	Book	Earliest existing copies	Time gap	Number of copies
John	John	c. AD 130	50-plus years	Fragments
The rest of the New Testament writers	The rest of the New Testament books	c. AD 200 (books)	100 years	
		c. AD 250 (most of New Testament)	150 years	
		c. AD 325 (complete New Testament)	225 years	5600-plus Greek manuscripts
		c. AD 366–384 (Latin Vulgate translation)	284 years	
		c. AD 400–500 (other translations)	400 years	19,000-plus translated manuscripts
		TOTALS	50–400 years	24,900-plus manuscripts

We can be confident that the text of the New Testament has been handed down over the centuries with precision and accuracy. In other words, we can be assured that what was written down initially is what we have today.

But a more basic question arises. Were the words from God recorded exactly as he intended? When these inspired writers were recording historical events, were they chronologically close to those events, so we can have confidence in the accuracy of what they wrote?

Many ancient writings adhere only loosely to the facts of the events they report. Some highly regarded authors of the ancient world, for example, report events that took place many years before they were born and in countries they had never visited. While their accounts may be largely factual, historians admit that greater credibility must be granted to writers who were both geographically and chronologically close to the events they report.

With that in mind, look at the loving care God took when he inspired the writing of the New Testament. The overwhelming weight of scholarship confirms that the accounts of Jesus' life, the history of the early church, and the letters that form the bulk of the New Testament were all written by men who were either eyewitnesses to the events they recorded or contemporaries of eyewitnesses. God selected Matthew, Mark, and John to write three of the four Gospels. These were men who could say such things as, "This report is from an eyewitness giving an accurate account" (John 19:35). He spoke through Luke the physician to record the third Gospel and the book of Acts. Luke, a meticulous and careful writer, used as "source material the reports circulating among us from the early disciples and other eyewitnesses of what God [did] in fulfillment of his promises" (Luke 1:2 NLT).

God could have spoken through anyone, from anywhere, to write his words about Christ. But to give us additional confidence in the truth, he worked through eyewitnesses such as John, who said, "We are telling you about what we ourselves have actually seen and heard" (1 John 1:3). He worked through Peter, who declared, "We did not follow cunningly devised fables when we made known to you the power and coming of our Lord Jesus Christ, but were eyewitnesses of His majesty" (2 Peter 1:16 NKJV). And whom did he choose as his most prolific writer? The apostle Paul, whose dramatic conversion from persecutor of Christians to planter of churches made him perhaps the most credible witness of all!

But God didn't stop there. Those through whom he transmitted his inspired Word were also apostles. These men could rely on their own eyewitness experiences, and they could appeal to the firsthand knowledge of their contemporaries, even their most rabid opponents (see Acts 2:32; 3:15; 13:31; 1 Corinthians 15:3-8). They not only said, "Look, we saw this," or "We heard that," but they were also so confident in what they wrote as to say, in effect, "Check it out," "Ask around," and "You know it as well as I do!"

Ample evidence exists to suggest that God was very selective in the people he chose to record his words—they were people who for the most part had firsthand knowledge of key events and who were credible channels to record and convey exactly those truths he wanted us to know. You can be confident when you read the New Testament as well as the rest of the Bible that you have a reliable transmission of what God inspired.*

* For a more comprehensive treatment of the reliability of the New Testament see *More Evidence That Demands a Verdict,* chapter 3.

67.

WHAT IS THE DIFFERENCE BETWEEN THE CHRISTIAN BIBLE AND THE JEWISH BIBLE?

The Christian Bible contains both the Old Testament and the New Testament. Some people say the Jewish Bible is the Christian Bible without the New Testament. Is that true? What is the Jewish or Hebrew Bible, and how does it differ from the Christian Bible?

The Jewish Bible is often referred to as the Torah. In the narrowest sense the Torah refers to the first five books of the Bible. In the broader sense, the Torah includes all Jewish law and tradition.

Contemporary Jews do not consider that they have an Old Testament. What Christians refer to as the Old Testament, the Jewish people would call the Written Torah or the *Tanakh*. Christians often refer to the Written Torah as the Hebrew Bible. The Hebrew Bible contains the same text as our Old Testament, but in a slightly different order. The Hebrew Bible ends with the historical books of Ezra-Nehemiah and Chronicles. The Christian Old Testament ends with the prophecies of Haggai, Zechariah, and Malachi.

Jesus read and taught from the Written Torah or Hebrew Bible. But at that time the Jewish religious leaders also quoted the Oral Torah. The Pharisees of Jesus' day believed that it contained the unwritten instructions given to Moses by God to help his people understand the laws and regulations and how to interpret and apply them. These traditions were then passed down orally from one generation to another.

The Pharisees taught that the Oral Torah carried the same authority as the Written Torah. And in Mark 7 we have an encounter between Jesus and the Pharisees about the Oral Torah. Jesus said, "You ignore God's law and substitute your own tradition [Oral Torah]...You skillfully sidestep God's law in order to hold on to your own tradition [Oral Torah]" (Mark 7:8-9). Jesus didn't necessarily condemn all aspects of the oral law, but he made it clear that the God-inspired Scripture (the Written Law) gave context to the Oral Law and that Scripture superseded the Oral Law.

By AD 200 the Oral Torah was written down in a document called the *Mishnah*. Additional commentaries elaborating on the Oral Torah or *Mishnah* were continually being added to by rabbis. These commentaries were known as the *Gemara*. They were written down and completed by AD 500. The *Gemara* and the *Mishnah* together are known as the Talmud. The Talmud deals with widely diverse subjects like agricultural laws, financial laws, issues of marriage, divorce, and contracts, laws dealing with ritual purity, impurity, sacrifices, and the temple. Today the Talmud contains more than 6000 folio pages and references and gives credit to over 2000 scholars or teachers.

So the Jewish Bible is more complex and expanded than the Christian Bible. Yet if you narrow the focus of the Jewish Bible to just the Written Torah, our present Old Testament is the equivalent to the Jewish Hebrew Bible.

68.

WHAT IS THE DIFFERENCE BETWEEN THE BIBLE AND THE QUR'AN?

Christianity and Islam are both monotheistic religions that believe in one almighty creator. The Muslims' holy book—the Qur'an—teaches creation, the existence of angels, that Jesus was a sinless, virgin-born prophet from God, and that there is a heaven, a hell, and a day of judgment. So with all these similarities, what are the differences between the Bible and the Qur'an?

Muslims believe the Qur'an is a revelation from God (*Allah*) that began to be verbally transmitted through the angel Gabriel to Muhammad when he was 40 years old (AD 610). They say that over a 23-year period Muhammad received these messages, which he precisely memorized. Shortly after his death (AD 632) the Qur'an was compiled into a single book. Today it is divided into 114 chapters, or *suras*, and is about the length of the Christian New Testament. Muslims consider the Qur'an in the original Arabic text to be the literal word of God. They believe it provides divine guidance for all humanity. They say Muhammad was God's last prophet, superseding Christ, and that the Qur'an is God's final revelation to us all.

THE QUR'AN ON GOD

The distinguishing characteristic of Islam and the Qur'an is the unity and transcendence of Allah or God. To become a Muslim one must confess the *shahadah*: "There is no God but Allah, and Muhammad is his messenger." Yet the God of the Qur'an is not the same as the God of the Bible.

The Qur'an does portray God as being eternal, all powerful, all knowing, holy, just, loving, and merciful. However, unlike the Bible, the Qur'an claims these are characteristics of God's will rather than his nature. That is to say, God may be called good because he causes good, but goodness is not the essence of his character. The Bible, on the other hand, teaches God is good because his very nature and character are holy, just, and right.*

---

* See "What Is God Really Like?" on page 39.

The Qur'an also teaches that Jesus is not God's Son, that he did not die on the cross for our sins, nor did he rise from the grave physically three days later. It additionally teaches a unitarian view of God rather than the Trinitarian view of the Bible. To believe that there is more than one person in the Godhead is idolatry to a Muslim.

THE SIX BASIC DOCTRINES

The Qur'an espouses six basic Muslim doctrines:

1. There is one and only one God.
2. There have been many prophets of God, including Abraham, Moses, Jesus, and Muhammad.
3. Allah created angels (*jinn*), some being good and others evil.
4. The Qur'an is God's complete and final revelation.
5. A day of judgment for all is coming, followed by heaven for the faithful and hell for the infidels.
6. God has full knowledge of and exercises predestination (*qadar*) over all that occurs in life.

THE QUR'AN ON SALVATION

The Qur'an explains that salvation—a place in paradise after death—is based on Allah's forgiveness: "To those who believe and do deeds of righteousness hath Allah promised forgiveness and a great reward" (Sura 5:9). The hope of life after death for a Muslim is based on whether their good deeds will outweigh their bad deeds and that Allah will be merciful.*[48] Yet what distinguishes the Bible from the Qur'an is how a person is made right with God and obtains eternal life.

The New Testament (with which Muslims disagree) teaches that

- "The wages of sin is death, but the free gift of God is eternal life through Christ Jesus our Lord" (Romans 6:23).
- "God loved the world so much that he gave his one and only

---

* This belief that our good works are what really matters to God is also held by the majority of today's professed Christians. One study among professed Christians in North America revealed that 81 percent said the essence of the Christian faith was "trying harder to follow the rules described in the Bible."

Son, so that everyone who believes in him will not perish but have eternal life" (John 3:16).

- "God paid a ransom to save you...And the ransom he paid was not mere gold or silver. It was the precious blood of Christ, the sinless, spotless Lamb of God...Through Christ you have come to trust in God. And you have placed your faith and hope in God because he raised Christ from the dead" (1 Peter 1:18-19,21).

- "It is by grace you have been saved, through faith—and this is not from yourself, it is the gift of God" (Ephesians 2:8 NIV).

- "Can we boast, then, that we have done anything to be accepted by God? No, because our acquittal is not based on good deeds. It is based on faith [in Jesus]. So we are made right with God through faith and not by obeying the law" (Romans 3:27-28).

The fundamental differences between the Qur'an and the Bible are in the Bible's revelation of 1) who God is (his holy and righteous character and nature), 2) how he deals with sin (his plan of salvation through Christ's atoning sacrifice), and 3) how humans gain a relationship with him (made his children by grace through faith in Christ).

69.

WHAT IS THE DIFFERENCE BETWEEN THE CHRISTIAN BIBLE AND THE BOOK OF MORMON?

The term *Mormons* is the common designation for those who are members of the Church of Jesus Christ of Latter-day Saints (LDS), which has its headquarters in Salt Lake City, Utah. In 1827 Mormon founder Joseph Smith claimed to be informed by an angel named Moroni about a set of gold plates buried in a hill in present-day New York. These plates were said to have ancient writings engraved on them. Smith said he uncovered these plates and then translated and published them as the Book of Mormon in 1830. So how does the Book of Mormon differ from the Christian Bible?

The LDS church bases its beliefs not just on the Book of Mormon. Joseph Smith also claimed to have had an encounter with Jesus in which Jesus revealed many things to him. These revelations were published in the Doctrine and Covenants. The accounts of Smith's interaction with Jesus and his story of discovering gold plates are found in a third book, entitled Pearl of Great Price. These three documents, along with the Bible, form the basis of LDS beliefs and continuing revelations. However, the LDS officially consider the Book of Mormon as the "most correct" book of scripture. Since the death of Joseph Smith in 1844 these documents have been supplemented by other revelations that the LDS church says have been given to its leaders.

The Book of Mormon is written in a King-James-Bible historic style and tells about two ancient civilizations that supposedly migrated to the American continent. The first group were said to be refugees from the Tower of Babel and the second group came from Jerusalem around 600 BC. The first group was eventually destroyed because of their corruption. The second group, under the leadership of a man named Nephi, was made up of God-fearing Jews, and they prospered. However, some of the people ceased to worship the true God and they received the curse of dark skin—these people were said to be Native Americans, earlier called "Indians."

The Book of Mormon claims that after Jesus' resurrection he visited America and revealed himself to the followers of Nephi. Eventually this group was destroyed by the "Indians" around AD 428. This history was written on gold plates. And it was these plates that Joseph Smith said he found and translated as the Book of Mormon.

TEACHINGS OF THE MORMON SCRIPTURES

Mormons believe the Bible is true "insofar as it is correctly translated." But they also accept their three church writings as God-inspired. Additionally, Mormons believe their church leaders continue to receive God-inspired revelations. So, in essence, new "revelations from God" supersede previous revelations.

The Book of Mormon, the Doctrine and Covenants, Pearl of Great Price, and the continuing revelations of the LDS church leaders form Mormon theology and teachings. Both the LDS church as an institution and its members present themselves as a part of the Christian faith and actually believe they are the only true church. The LDS church expresses a healthy emphasis on families and moral values derived from the Bible. The church has extensive welfare programs for its members and a compassionate missionary operation around the world. This creates a positive image and is attracting large numbers of people to the LDS church. The theology of the Mormons, however, is not that of Christianity taught from the Old and New Testament Scriptures. For example, the LDS church teaches the following:

- There are three separate Gods—Father, Son, and Holy Spirit—rather than one God in three persons as the Bible teaches (see Matthew 28:19).

- God the Father was once a human and today has flesh and bones rather than a being a spirit (as Jesus said in John 4:24).

- Humans are destined to evolve into godhood. The Mormon saying is "As man is, God once was: as God is, man may become." The Bible teaches we are to be transformed into God's likeness, not evolve into godhood (see Ephesians 4:23-24).

- Works are the basis of salvation and determining what kind of position and place you have in heaven, rather than being justified by grace through faith in Jesus (see Ephesians 2:8 and Romans 3:27-28).

- Scripture is not the final revelation of God—rather, the leaders of the LDS church receive continuing revelations that are equal to and even supersede the Old and New Testament Scriptures. But the Bible teaches that Scripture is the inspired revelation of God (see 2 Timothy 3:16-17).*

To sum up, the Book of Mormon and the other writings of the LDS church differ significantly from the Christian Bible.

---

* See "What Does It Mean that the Bible Is Inspired?" on page 148.

70.

HOW IS THE ROMAN CATHOLIC BIBLE DIFFERENT FROM THE PROTESTANT BIBLE?

The Christian tradition includes the Roman Catholic, Orthodox, and Protestant traditions. While there are significant differences in the theology of Roman Catholics and Protestants, is there likewise a difference in the Bibles of the two traditions? Do Roman Catholics have a Bible different from that of Protestants?

The Roman Catholic Bible contains 14 more books in its Old Testament than does the Protestant Bible. Other than this, the Roman Catholic and Protestant Bibles contain the same books, though the two groups may translate some passages differently. So what are these 14 books, and why do Roman Catholics accept them and Protestants do not?

No later than 400 BC, the last books of the Hebrew Old Testament were written. They were Malachi, written around 450 to 430 BC, and Chronicles, written no later than 400 BC. As early as the 300s BC, and certainly no later than 150 BC, all 39 books of the Old Testament had been written, collected, and recognized as Scripture by Jewish leaders. In the Hebrew text these 39 books were originally divided up as 24 books: 5 books of the Law, 8 Prophets, and 11 Writings. Today the Protestant Bible simply divides these 24 books differently to get 39.

Around 250 to 150 BC the officially recognized Hebrew text by Jewish leaders was translated into Greek. It is called the Septuagint and is sometimes designated by the Roman numeral 70: "LXX." This meant there were now a Hebrew Old Testament and the Septuagint. During the same time period various writers composed historical stories of the Jewish people and various additions or clarifications to the Old Testament books of Esther and Daniel. This was well after the official close of the Old Testament. However, 14 such writings were added to the Greek translation, the

Septuagint. They were First and Second Esdras, Tobit, Judith, additions to Esther, Wisdom of Solomon, Ecclesiasticus, Baruch, Susanna, Bel and the Dragon and Songs of the Three Hebrew Children (both additions to Daniel), the Prayers of Manasseh, and First and Second Maccabees. These books are referred to as the Apocrypha.

CONTROVERSY ABOUT THE APOCRYPHA

The great scholar Jerome (about AD 340–420) began his work of translating the Hebrew Old Testament into Latin under Pope Damasus. The translation was called the Latin Vulgate. Jerome rejected the Apocrypha as part of the canon. Throughout the early church and into the Reformation period many scholars also rejected the Apocrypha. But at the Counter-Reformation Council of Trent the Roman Catholic Church officially recognized the Apocrypha as Scripture and gave them full canonical status (AD 1546).

The Roman Catholic Church recognized these 14 additional books in part to strengthen certain doctrines that were being undermined by the Reformers. The book of Tobit, for example, taught the atoning virtues of good works, and Second Maccabees supported the Roman Catholic doctrines of intercession of the saints and purgatory.

The Jewish leaders, early church scholars, and the Reformers rejected the canonicity of the Apocrypha, and thus the Bible of Protestants excluded these books. There were numerous reasons apart from the above mentioned that the Apocrypha was not considered God-inspired. These reasons include the following:

- None of the 14 added books claimed divine inspiration, and in fact some actually disclaimed it.

- Noted historians and philosophers rejected them; namely Philo of Alexandria (20 BC–AD 40), Josephus (AD 30–100), and the Jewish scholars of Jamnia (AD 90).

- None of the New Testament writers ever once quoted the Apocrypha, although hundreds of quotes were made of the Hebrew Old Testament in the form of the Septuagint.

- Jesus never recognized the Apocryphal books or quoted from them.

WHAT JESUS CONFIRMED

It is Jesus' statements in Scripture that are perhaps the strongest indicator that the Apocrypha is not to be considered God's inspired Word. He acknowledged the completeness of the entire Hebrew text (the original 24 books of the Old Testament excluding the Apocrypha) when he said that "everything written about me in the law of Moses [the first five books] and the prophets [the eight books] and in the Psalms [the eleven writings] must be fulfilled" (Luke 24:44).

Additionally Jesus referred to the first and last martyrs within the Hebrew text when he used the phrase "from the murder of Abel to the murder of Zechariah" (Luke 11:51). By doing this he was referring to the first book of the Old Testament (Genesis) to the last book of the Hebrew text (Chronicles). This clearly shows that Jesus confirmed the authority and inspiration of the 24 books that make up our 39 Old Testament books today. He excluded all other writings, including the Apocrypha, when he referred to the God-inspired Scriptures.

God spoke through Moses and cautioned that God's Word should not be added to or subtracted from: "You must not add anything to them or subtract anything from them" (Deuteronomy 12:32). The apostle John gave a similar warning about the book he was inspired by God to write: "If anyone adds anything to what is written here, God will add to that person the plagues described in this book" (Revelation 22:18). Jewish leaders and the apostles of Jesus in the first century were protective of God's written revelation and rightfully so. And we can be confident that what we have in the 66 books of the Protestant Bible—nothing more and nothing less—is God's inspired Word to us.

71

WHEN WAS THE BIBLE TRANSLATED INTO OTHER LANGUAGES?

Those who were inspired by God to write down his Word wrote in Hebrew and Aramaic (in the Old Testament) and Greek (in the New Testament). We have discussed how scribes and manuscript copyists preserved those writings by carefully duplicating them word for word.* But of course not everyone could read Hebrew, Aramaic, or Greek. So the Bible was translated into other languages. When were these translations made, and into what languages?

The Bible has now been translated into more than 2400 languages. And over the years this task has required multitudes of translators and scholars. The very first translation of the Bible (the Old Testament) was made into Greek, and it is called the *Septuagint*. It was translated from the Jewish Hebrew and Aramaic text that today makes up our 39 Old Testament books. Finished around 250 to 150 BC, it was the Old Testament that the Greek-speaking world read in Jesus' time. Jesus quoted from it as well from as the Hebrew text.

TRANSLATIONS DURING THE TIME OF THE EARLY CHURCH

Many years later other scholars translated the Old Testament into Greek. Some of these manuscripts are in existence today. The *Codex Sinaiticus* and *Codex Vaticanus,* two such manuscripts, date to approximately AD 330. Today they reside in the British Museum and the Vatican Library in Rome respectively.

The *Coptic Version* was made around AD 350. It was translated from the Greek into a language called Coptic, which was a version of Late Egyptian that was written in mostly Greek characters. At this same time period the *Ethiopic Version* and *Gothic Version: Codex Argenteus* were made. We

---

*he Old Testament Historically Reliable?" on page 192 and "Is the New Testament Historically Reliable?"

212

know there were Ethiopian Christians as early as the event reported in Acts 8:26-36. The Goths lived in the area of present-day Hungary and Romania.

The Latin *Vulgate* was translated by the scholar Jerome beginning in AD 382. It took him 25 years to translate the entire Old Testament from the Hebrew and Greek translation into Latin, as he was appointed to do by Roman Catholic Pope Damasus. The Latin Vulgate is said to be the first book that Johannes Gutenberg printed in 1455.

Beginning in the fourth century the Hebrew and Greek Bible was also translated into such languages as Armenian, Slavic, Syriac (a late version of Aramaic), Bahairic (a dialect of Coptic), Arabic, Anglo-Saxon, Persian, and Frankish. At least a portion of those ancient manuscript translations still exist today.

ENGLISH TRANSLATIONS

Translations into English or its precursor languages began to be made in the fifth century, starting with the Anglo-Saxon version. The first person to translate the entire Bible into the English language was John Wycliffe (1329–1384). Wycliffe's English translation was the only English language Bible for 145 years. In 1525 William Tyndale created the Tyndale Version of the English Bible. Tyndale was perhaps the greatest of modern English translators of the Bible. Other English versions made in the next hundred years or so included the Coverdale Version (1535), the Great Bible (1539), the Geneva Bible (1557), and the well-known Authorized Version, commonly known as the King James Version (1611).

The King James Version of the Bible became one of the most popular versions in the English-speaking world and is still the preferred translation for many. In the late nineteenth century the Church of England felt a revision and updating was needed. The Revised King James Version was complete in 1885.

The American Standard Version (1901) was yet another version of the King James Version. From that point to present there have been over two dozen different English translations published, with hundreds more in other languages. Following are some of the most popular English translations and paraphrases of the past 50 or so years.

- The Revised Standard Version (1952, revised 1971)
- The Amplified Bible (1965)

- The New English Bible (1970)
- The New American Standard Bible (1971, revised 1995)
- The Living Bible (1971)
- Good News for Modern Man (1976)
- The New International Version (1978, revised 2011)
- The New King James Version (1982)
- The New Century Bible (1988)
- The Message (1994)
- God's Word Translation (1995)
- The New Living Translation (1996, revised 2004)
- The Holman Christian Standard Bible (1999, revised 2009)
- The English Standard Version (2001, revised 2011)

For a more comprehensive list of versions and translations of the Bible in various languages, visit BibleGateway.com and go to "available versions."

72.

Have Any Translations of the Bible Been Inspired?

The 66 books of the Bible were written by over 40 different authors over a 1500-year span. And since that time scribes and copiers of the ancient manuscripts have accurately copied the Scripture in their original language (Hebrew, Aramaic, and Greek) for centuries up until the modern printing press.*

From these ancient Bible manuscripts scholars then have translated the Scripture into various languages—over 2400 languages to date. The question is, were these various translators inspired of God to accurately interpret the words and meaning of the Hebrew, Aramaic, and Greek into other languages?

There is no doubt many of the translators were godly people and passionate about seeing God's Word made available to other people of the world. And they no doubt worked carefully to accurately translate the Bible. Yet they were not God-inspired as were those who originally penned the words of God.

When the Bible says that "all Scripture is inspired by God" (2 Timothy 3:16) it means the words were "God-breathed" through those who penned the Scripture.† So when the original authors of Scripture wrote, they were writing the words of God. When translators make translations, they are engaged in a literary and grammatical language exercise. It is certainly an important one and one perhaps even guided by God. Yet it is not

---

* See "Is the Old Testament Historically Reliable?" on page 192 and "Is the New Testament Historically Reliable?" on page 196.

† See "What Does It Mean that the Bible Is Inspired?" on page 148.

as though he is giving a translator the precise words to write down in order to convey the precise meaning of the Hebrew or Greek words in Scripture.

So if translators are not inspired by God in their work, then they can translate words incorrectly. And that could mean that some passages in various languages would be mistranslated. Is that the case? This is the subject of the next question.

73

IF BIBLE TRANSLATORS MADE MISTAKES, WOULDN'T THAT MAKE THE BIBLE INACCURATE?

In the last question we stated that Bible translators were not and are not inspired by God when they translate Scripture from Hebrew and Greek into other languages. And if that is the case, wouldn't that mean that some translations could be mistranslated and inaccurate?

Today when a publisher or institution decides to release a translation of the Bible they do so with great care. Typically a Bible translation committee is formed. That committee then recruits a team of scholars from various theological backgrounds, usually seminary professors with extensive insight and experience in Hebrew, Aramaic, or Greek. For example, when Tyndale House Publishers set out to create the New Living Translation (NLT) they created six teams of over 90 scholars to focus on their areas of expertise: Pentateuch, Historical Books, Prophets, Gospels, and so on. Then they took years to carefully translate the NLT.

COMPARING AND CONSIDERING

But does this mean that every translation is done accurately? Do the translators sometimes convey a different meaning than the original Hebrew or Greek intended? The translators are human and have sometimes chosen words and phrases that are incorrect or less accurate. That is why people prefer certain translations over others—some Bible versions do a better job of translating than others.* Of course, that is why teams are formed and careful review is made—to avoid misinterpretation.

But it is also important for you to compare various English translations with others and consult commentaries and word-study references. There are excellent Hebrew and Greek Bible dictionaries, such as W.E. Vine's *Expository Dictionary of New Testament Words* and *An Expository Dictionary*

---

* See " How Do I Choose an English Translation that Is Accurate?" on page 219.

*of Old Testament Words.** By choosing a highly respected translation, comparing a translation with others, and referring to commentaries and a Bible dictionary, you can be confident in getting an accurate rendering of Scripture. But how do you choose an English translation that is accurate? That is the topic of the next question.

74

HOW DO I CHOOSE AN ENGLISH TRANSLATION THAT IS ACCURATE?

There are over 20 English translations of the Bible on the market. And if some of these translations are more accurate than others, how do you choose the best one?

It is true that some translations are more accurate or more closely rendered to the original Hebrew or Greek language than others. And while that is true, translation accuracy is a complicated issue.

TRANSLATION VS. PARAPHRASE

First, let's clarify between a translation and paraphrase. A Bible translation is produced when the translators render each passage of Scripture from the original text of the Old Testament and New Testament. Translators will often translate the Old Testament into English from the Masoretic text of the Hebrew Bible represented in the *Biblia Hebraica Stuttgartensia* (1977). They will often make comparisons to the Dead Sea Scrolls, the Septuagint and other Greek translations of the Old Testament, the Samaritan Pentateuch, the Latin Vulgate, and so on. The English New Testament is often translated from two standard editions of the Greek New Testament: *Novum Testamentum Graece* (NA, 27th edition, 1993) and *The Greek New Testament* (United Bible Societies, 4th revised edition, 1993).

Paraphrases, on the other hand, are often done by one person and represent his or her rephrasing of a translation. While these may be helpful, they will inevitably reflect the viewpoint of the one making the paraphrase.

APPROACHES TO TRANSLATION

Translations also differ because of the translation theory they utilize. This will, in some people's opinion, dictate the accuracy of the translation. Some prefer a translation dictated by what is called "formal equivalence"— a "literal" or "word-for-word" translation. In this approach the translator attempts to render each word into English, with the goal of preserving the sentence structure and syntax of the original language. While this would seem to be the best approach to get the most accurate translation, a pure formal-equivalence translation would be almost unintelligible in English. So some interpretation is necessary, but when the word-for-word approach is taken the result may still give the reader difficulty in determining a passage's meaning. The New American Standard Bible (NASB) largely used this approach.

The second translation approach is called "dynamic equivalence," "functional equivalence," or "thought-for-thought." This approach is to translate in English the closest natural equivalent to the message expressed in the original scriptural text, both in meaning and style. The end result often creates a more readable and naturally flowing text. The New International Version (NIV) largely used this approach.

Both of these translation theories have their strengths. The formal-equivalence can get at the original language syntax and is often preferred by Bible scholars and teachers. The dynamic-equivalence is often more readable and the meaning of the text more apparent to the contemporary reader.

One could argue for one translation over the other and make a case for those translations that are less accurate. And critics of various English translations have done just that. But we are not here to side with any one critic or defend this translation or that one. Every one of them is subject to mistranslation, and no translation is inspired by God.*

MAKING YOUR CHOICE

Yet the question remains—how to choose an accurate and readable Bible translation. The best advice on choosing a good one is to first ask a Christian leader you highly respect, like your pastor or a seminary professor. Find out which one they use and which one they would recommend for you. Second, check out the translation team that produced the translation you are looking at and discover the approach they followed. This information should be in the preface or introduction of the Bible. Often the team members are listed and you can verify their credentials and determine what seminaries and groups they are affiliated with.

Ultimately you may end up using multiple translations, like we do. A version like the New American Standard Bible (NASB) might be used

---

* See "Have Any Translations of the Bible Been Inspired?" on page 215.

for study since it provides a more literal word translation. Yet some feel its sentence structure and wording doesn't always lend itself to public reading or devotional use. In that case you might lean toward the New International Version (NIV), which renders passages into a clear, natural English. You might even consider a *comparative* study Bible, which provides four or so translations in one Bible. Various online services allow you to also read multiple translations side by side.

Ultimately your choice will come down to personal preference. However, you will want to be sure your English Bible translation is reliable as well as readable.

75.

WHY ARE THERE SO MANY ENGLISH TRANSLATIONS OF THE BIBLE?

The English Bible is certainly a popular book. Some English translation is sold in practically every bookstore in every city in North America. Nearly every online book retailer sells at least one. And there are over 20 English versions to choose from. You might ask, "Why so many?"

In recent years Christian leaders have encouraged Christians to read and study their Bibles. This has created a demand for God's Word, and many publishers have responded. And to increase Bible circulation, publishers have targeted various groups. Publishing houses have released such Bibles as *The Apologetics Study Bible, The Men's Study Bible, The Women's Study Bible, The Apologetics Study Bible for Students, The Praise and Worship Study Bible, The One Year Bible, The Note Makers Bible, The Children's Bible*...and the list goes on. There are large-print Bibles, thin-line Bibles, leather-bound, hardback, paperback, online, and so on. Then there are highly respected pastors and scholars who have come out with study Bibles that incorporate their commentary and notes.

In the effort to distribute Bibles, publishers and other groups have either acquired or commissioned translations that appeal to all the above groups and more. Consequently, we have many English translations and Bible formats from which to choose.*

---

* See "How Do I Choose an English Translation that Is Accurate?" on page 219.

76.

WHAT ARE THE RESOURCES I NEED TO ACCURATELY INTERPRET THE BIBLE?

The Bible was written in different time periods and in cultures very different from ours. Let's face it—the Bible isn't an easy read. In question 60, "How Do You Correctly Interpret the Bible?" we discussed how we needed to understand the meaning of words and the context of those words. But without help from experienced scholars, that can be a real challenge. So what are the resources needed to accurately interpret the Bible?

We will mention five tools or resources that will greatly aid you in your study.

Definitions and word studies. The most effective way to interpret a word from the Bible—that is, to know the meaning of it—is to look it up in a dictionary. Usually a Bible dictionary will give you an expanded biblical definition of a word. A good Bible dictionary gives you not only the definition and the background of a word, but also its Old Testament and New Testament usages. Search the Internet for "Bible Dictionary" and you find free sites through which you can look up most words in the Bible. On such sites you will also see a number of resources to purchase if you are seeking a hard-copy version of a Bible dictionary or a software program. Note that dictionaries will often give multiple meanings, so be sure to consider the context when determining the particular meaning.

There are also concordances with Hebrew and Greek lexicons, which also give meanings of the original languages of Scripture. One of the most widely used is Strong's Concordance. Search "Greek Dictionary" online and you will find a variety of resources in print, online, and in software. Also check with your local Christian bookstore.

Reference books. We have mentioned before the need to cross-reference Scripture passages and words. There are resources that provide valuable information on Bible history and information about life, thinking, and attitudes in Bible times. They include study Bibles, Bible encyclopedias, commentaries, and atlases. These materials give us the scholarly insights of experts—the observations of people who have spent a lifetime researching and studying subjects we may never be able to explore for ourselves. Over the centuries men like W.E. Vine and James Strong, and many other devout and dedicated Christians, have compiled written resources that can be highly valuable to us in understanding how to accurately interpret the meaning of God's Word.

Study Bibles. A study Bible is one of the most useful study tools you can own. Many such Bibles contain wide-ranging information you would have no way of knowing unless you were a Bible scholar or a serious student. A good study Bible may replace many of the types of reference books listed here. Many of them include a brief Scripture commentary, introductions to books of the Bible and summaries of them, charts, maps, graphs, sidebars, textual footnotes, chain references, dictionaries, concordances, and other help and information that may often eliminate the need to turn to other resources.

Commentaries. A Bible commentary is exactly what the term implies. It contains the comments of a Bible scholar or scholars explaining the meaning of Bible passages. Commentaries can be in-depth, verse-by-verse multivolume works or single-volume works on the entire Bible, which treat the basic themes of chapters and highlight certain verses.

Computer and online resources. We have mentioned that a good study Bible can fill the place of many of the resources we have identified so far. The same is true with online and computer software Bible aids. An excellent example of an online Bible resource is Biblegateway.com, which is superb for finding specific scriptures and linking references. By just typing in your reference or a word or two, you can use it as a concordance, or to look up the text of any verse in the Bible in nearly any English version.

If you obtain a Bible software program to install on your computer you can essentially get every resource we've mentioned above. Such programs will have a Bible dictionary, a Bible encyclopedia, the complete text of the Bible in a number of versions with several ways of accessing them, cross-referencing tools, Bible-study helps, charts, maps, and commentaries. In addition they often have many visual features, including photos, illustrations, animated clips of many Bible incidents, and archaeological information.

There are a number of Bible software programs such as Logos Bible, Biblesoft, BibleWorks, iLumina, and others. Check these out online or contact your local Christian bookstore.

77.

How Do I Personally
Experience the Bible?

One key emphasis we have made throughout this book is that God is relational and that he "is passionate about his relationship with you" (Exodus 34:14 NLT). And he has given his children his Spirit and his Word to allow each of us to experience that relationship. But how do we experience the Bible in order to deepen our relationship with God?

Back when I (Sean) was in college a few Christian friends invited me to their Bible-study group. As a single college student I wanted to develop the discipline of getting into God's Word with my fellow classmates. But what struck me was the lens through which a couple of my buddies read practically every verse. They always seemed to have at least three questions they had to ask about each passage:

1. What sin here needs to be avoided?
2. What commandment here needs to be obeyed?
3. What part of my life needs to be changed?

It is not that we shouldn't avoid sin or understand what biblical commands we need to obey. But my friends seemed to view God as an inspecting and disappointed God. And when we see him through this type of lens we tend to distort his truth. Paul prayed for the Christ-followers in Ephesus that God would "give you the Spirit of wisdom and revelation, so that you may know [Jesus] better...that the eyes of your heart may be enlightened in order that you may know the hope to which he has called you" (Ephesians 1:17-18 NIV).

God has given you his Word, in part, so you can know Jesus better and have frequent fresh encounters with him to experience just how much he cares for you. Peter encourages you to "give all your worries and cares to God, for he cares about you" (1 Peter 5:7). But you may at times wonder if Jesus' compassion can be experienced personally, as was the case with those who encountered him while he was on earth. You may think, *Well, he did make himself real and relevant to those he encountered, but how can his compassion be real and relevant to me through reading his Word?*

GOD'S INVITATION TO YOU

The key to experiencing your Bible is viewing God's Book as your personal invitation to know him better. With this mind-set, consider asking the following questions when studying the Scriptures:

- How does this scripture relate to loving God more deeply with all my heart, soul, and mind?
- How does this scripture relate to loving others as God loves me?
- How does this passage reveal the caring, compassionate heart of Jesus?
- What is Jesus wanting me to experience from him right now?
- What about God's plans and purpose do I see that relates to me in this passage?
- How does God see people differently than I do?
- How does my heart respond to this relational God, including his loving discipline?
- How does God want me to respond to those who are lost and without him?

Through the miraculous power of God's Spirit, Jesus wants us to experience his Word on a daily basis. He wants his mind to be our mind. He wants his life to become our life. He prayed to his Father for both his disciples and for us, saying,

> They are not part of this world any more than I am. Make them pure and holy by teaching them your words of truth...My prayer for all of them is that they will be one, just as you and I are one, Father—that just as you are in me and I am in you, so they will be in us, and the world will believe you sent me (John 17:16-17,21 NLT).

Embrace the accepting and compassionate Jesus who is there to meet you at the point of your need. He wants you to experience him as you experience his Word.[49]

NOTES

1. Rich Deem, "Evidence for the Fine Tuning of the Universe," article accessed May 17, 2011, at www.godandscience.org/apologetics/designun.html.

2. William A. Dembski and Sean McDowell, *Understanding Intelligent Design* (Eugene, OR: Harvest House Publishers, 2008), 122-123, slightly adapted.

3. Hill Roberts and Mark Whorton, *Holman QuickSource Guide to Understanding Creation* (Nashville: B&H Publishing, 2008), 323.

4. Dembski and McDowell, 109-110, slightly adapted.

5. Dembski and McDowell, 133-134, slightly adapted; embedded citation from Michael Denton, *Evolution: A Theory in Crisis* (Chevy Chase, MD: Adler and Adler, 1986), 264.

6. Sean McDowell, *Ethix* (Nashville, TN: Broadman & Holman Publishers, 2006), 49-50; embedded citation from Fyodor Dostoyevsky, *The Brothers Karamazov* (New York, NY: Bantam Books, 1970), 95.

7. Adapted from Josh McDowell and Thomas Williams, *In Search of Certainty* (Wheaton, IL: Tyndale House Publishers, 2003), 46-47.

8. Josh McDowell and Sean McDowell, *More Than a Carpenter* (Wheaton, IL: Tyndale House Publishers, 2009), 161-162.

9. Zeina Karam and John Heilprin, "U.N. Says Children Tortured in Syria," *Akron* (Ohio) *Beacon Journal*, November 29, 2011.

10. "Age and Size of the Universe" at www.en.wikipedia.org/wiki/universe, 2009.

11. Richard Dawkins, *The God Delusion* (New York: Mariner, 2008), 51.

12. Jonalyn Grace Fincher, "Defending Feminity: Why Jesus Is Good News for Women," in *Apologetics for a New Generation,* Sean McDowell, gen. ed. (Eugene, OR: Harvest House Publishers, 2009), 223.

13. Fincher, 224-225.

14. J. Harold Ellens, *The Destructive Power of Religion: Violence in Judaism, Christianity and Islam* (Greenwood Publishing Group, 2007), accessed on September 8, 2011 and quoted at http://books.google.com/books?id=0fooSsaO6rMC&dq=the+destructive+power+of+religion+by+j+harold+ellens&source=gbs_navlinks_s.

15. Christopher Hitchens, *God Is Not Great: How Religion Poisons Everything* (New York: Twelve Books, 2007), 13.

16. F.W. Nietzsche, *The Antichrist*, tr. H.L. Mencken (Torrance, CA: The Noontide Press, 1980), 180.

17. Hitchens, 101.

18. J.I. Packer, *Knowing God*, 20th anniversary ed. (Downers Grove, IL: InterVarsity Press, 1993), 143.

19. Timothy Keller, *The Reason for God: Belief in an Age of Skepticism* (New York: Dutton, 2008), 76-77.

20. C.S. Lewis, *The Abolition of Man* (New York: Macmillan, 1947), 69.

21. As reported at www.thecomputerwizard.biz/lightning.htm.

22. Bart D. Ehrman, *God's Problem: How the Bible Fails to Answer Our Most Important Question—Why We Suffer* (New York: Harper Collins Publishers, 2008), as quoted in blog.beliefnet.com article "Bart Ehrman: How the Problem of Pain Ruined My Faith."

23. Institute of International Studies, *Perspectives on the World Christian Movement* (Pasadena, CA: William Carey Library, 2009), 362-364.

24. As quoted in Cathy Lynn Grossman, "Baylor Religion Survey Reveals Many See God Steering Economy," *USA Today*, September 20, 2011.

25. Dawkins, 117.

26. The Pew Forum on Religion and Public Life Washington DC Survey: "Many Americans Say Other Faiths Can Lead to Eternal Life," December 18, 2008, as reported at http://pewforum.org/Many-Americans-Say-Other-Faiths-Can-Lead-to-Eternal-Life.aspx.

27. Statistics taken from Alan Hirsch, *The Forgotten Ways* (Grand Rapids, MI: Brazos Press, 2006), 18.

28. Josh McDowell and Bill Wilson, *Evidence for the Historical Jesus* (Eugene, OR: Harvest House Publishers, 2011), 38.

29. McDowell and Wilson, 36.

30. McDowell and Wilson, 44.

31. McDowell and Wilson, 47.

32. McDowell and Wilson, 49-51.

33. For a detailed treatment of this prophecy, see Josh McDowell, *The New Evidence That Demands a Verdict* (Nashville: Thomas Nelson Publishers, 1999), 195-201.

34. As quoted in Ravi Zacharias and Norman Geisler, *Who Made God?* (Grand Rapids, MI: Zondervan, 2003), 97.

35. Adapted from Josh McDowell and Sean McDowell, *The Unshakable Truth* (Eugene, OR: Harvest House Publishers, 2010), 379-380.

36. McDowell and McDowell, *The Unshakable Truth,* 409-411.

37. McDowell and McDowell, *The Unshakable Truth,* 231-233.

38. McDowell and McDowell, *The Unshakable Truth,* 96.

39. Josh McDowell, *More Evidence That Demands a Verdict* (Nashville, TN: Thomas Nelson Publishers, 1999), 21-22.

40. McDowell, *More Evidence,* 26.

41. Josh McDowell and Sean McDowell, *Experience Your Bible* (Eugene, OR: Harvest House Publishers, 2012), 97.

42. McDowell and McDowell, *Experience Your Bible,* 68-70.

43. McDowell, *The New Evidence,* 74.

44. McDowell, *The New Evidence,* 79.

45. Adapted from McDowell, *The New Evidence,* chart, 38.

46. McDowell, *The New Evidence,* 38.

47. McDowell, *The New Evidence,* 38-39.

48. Barna Research Group, "Many Churchgoers and Faith Leaders Struggle to Define Spiritual Maturity" (Ventura, CA: The Barna Research Group, Ltd., 2008), 1, 3, at Barna.org website article #264.

49. Adapted from McDowell and McDowell, *Experience Your Bible*, chapters 3, 4, and 9.

ABOUT THE AUTHORS
AND THE JOSH McDOWELL MINISTRY

As a young man, **Josh McDowell** was a skeptic of Christianity. However, while at Kellogg College in Michigan, he was challenged by a group of Christian students to intellectually examine the claims of Jesus Christ. Josh accepted the challenge and came face-to-face with the reality that Jesus was in fact the Son of God, who loved him enough to die for him. Josh committed his life to Christ, and for 50 years he has shared with the world both his testimony and the evidence that God is real and relevant to our everyday lives.

Josh received a bachelor's degree from Wheaton College and a master's degree in theology from Talbot Theological Seminary in California. He has been on staff with Campus Crusade for Christ for almost 50 years. Josh and his wife, Dottie, have been married for more than 40 years and have four grown children and five grandchildren. They live in Southern California.

Sean McDowell is an educator, speaker, and author. He graduated summa cum laude from Talbot Theological Seminary with a double master's degree in philosophy and theology. He is the head of the Bible department at Capistrano Valley Christian School and is presently pursuing a PhD in apologetics and worldview studies at Southern Baptist Theological Seminary. You can read Sean's blog and contact him for speaking events at www.seanmcdowell.org.

Sean and his wife, Stephanie, have been married for more than ten years and have two children. They live in Southern California.

OTHER RESOURCES FROM
JOSH AND SEAN MCDOWELL

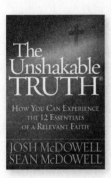

THE UNSHAKABLE TRUTH®
How You Can Experience the 12 Essentials of a Relevant Faith

As a Christian, you may feel unsure about what you believe and why. Maybe you wonder if your faith is even meaningful and credible.

Unpacking 12 biblical truths that define the core of Christian belief and Christianity's reason for existence, this comprehensive yet easy-to-understand handbook helps you discover

- the foundational truths about God, his Word, sin, Christ, the Trinity, the church, and six more that form the bedrock of Christian faith

- how you can live out these truths in relationship with God and others

- ways to pass each truth on to your family and the world around you

Biblically grounded, spiritually challenging, and full of practical examples and real-life stories, *The Unshakable Truth* is a resource applicable to every aspect of everyday life.

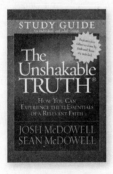

THE UNSHAKABLE TRUTH® STUDY GUIDE
This study guide offers you—or you and your group—a *relational experience* to discover...

- 12 foundational truths of Christianity—in sessions about God, his Word, the Trinity, Christ's atonement, his resurrection, his return, the church, and five more

- "Truth Encounter" exercises to actually help you live out these key truths

- "TruthTalk" assignments on ways to share the essentials of the faith with your family and others

Through twelve 15-minute Web-link videos, Josh and Sean McDowell draw on their own father-son legacy of faith to help you feel adequate to impart what you believe with confidence. *Includes instructions for group leaders.*

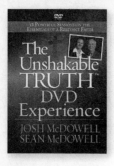

THE UNSHAKABLE TRUTH™ DVD EXPERIENCE
12 Powerful Sessions on the Essentials of a Relevant Faith

What do I believe, and why do I believe it? How is it relevant to my life? How do I live it out?

If you're asking yourself questions like these, you're not alone. In 12 quick, easy-to-grasp video sessions based on their book *The Unshakable Truth*, Josh and Sean McDowell give a solid introduction to the foundations of the faith.

Josh and Sean outline 12 key truths with clear explanations, compelling discussions, and provocative "on-the-street" interviews. And uniquely, they explain these truths *relationally*, showing you how living them out changes you and affects family and friends—everyone you encounter. *Helpful leader's directions included.*

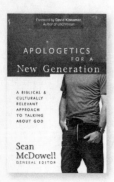

APOLOGETICS FOR A NEW GENERATION
A Biblical and Culturally Relevant Approach to Talking About God
Sean McDowell

This generation's faith is constantly under attack from the secular media, skeptical teachers, and unbelieving peers. You may wonder, *How can I help?*

Working with young adults every day, Sean McDowell understands their situation and shares your concern. His first-rate team of contributors shows how you can help members of the new generation plant their feet firmly on the truth. Find out how you can walk them through the process of...

- formulating a biblical worldview and applying scriptural principles to everyday issues

- articulating their questions and addressing their doubts in a safe environment

- becoming confident in their faith and effective in their witness

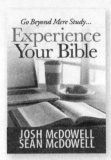

Go Beyond Mere Study...
EXPERIENCE YOUR BIBLE

In *Experience Your Bible,* Josh and Sean McDowell delve into God's original design for the Scriptures—revealing himself to you so you can experience him and a deepened relationship with others.

With this in mind, Josh and Sean show you how the Bible can radically transform your life:

- The only hope of a life of joy is in a relational experience with God. The Bible is designed to guide you into that kind of relationship.

- God wants you to relationally experience things like acceptance, security, and comfort with him and others...not just mechanically obey commands.

- Your encounter with God's book can become a journey into what relationships with God and others were meant to be.

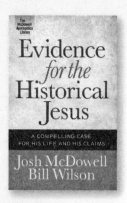

EVIDENCE FOR THE HISTORICAL JESUS
A Compelling Case for His Life and His Claims
Josh McDowell and Bill Wilson

After two years of intensive research, the agnostic Josh McDowell was convinced of the reliability of the historical evidence showing that Jesus of Nazareth existed and was precisely who He said He was—God in the flesh. Confronted by the living Lord, Josh accepted the offer of a relationship with Him.

In *Evidence for the Historical* Jesus, Josh teams with writer-researcher Bill Wilson to provide you with a thorough analysis to document that Jesus Christ actually walked on this earth—and that the New Testament accounts are incredibly reliable in describing His life. The authors' broad-ranging investigation examines

- the writings of ancient rabbis, martyrs, and early church leaders
- the evidence of the New Testament text
- historical geography and archaeology

Detailed and incisive but accessible, this volume will help you relate to people who distort or discount Christianity and its Founder. And it will strengthen your confidence in Jesus Christ and in the Scriptures that document His words, His life, and His love.